THE MONEY CODE

IMPROVE YOUR ENTIRE FINANCIAL LIFE RIGHT NOW

GREENLEAF
BOOK GROUP PRESS

ALSO BY JOE JOHN DURAN

Start It, Sell It & Make a Mint
20 Wealth-Creating Secrets for Business Owners

First Time Investor's Workbook
A Hands-On Guide to Implementing a Successful Investment Plan

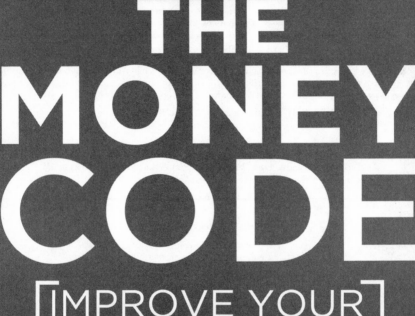

THE
MONEY
CODE

[IMPROVE YOUR
ENTIRE FINANCIAL LIFE
RIGHT NOW]

JOE JOHN DURAN, CFA

Published and distributed by Greenleaf Book Group Press
Austin, Texas
GBGPress.com

Artwork used to illustrate the Money Secrets reprinted with permission from Carl Richards and United Capital. Illustrations created by Carl Richards and Behavior Gap, BehaviorGap.com.

Cover design by Marlena Sigman

Publisher's Cataloging-In-Publication Data
(Prepared by The Donohue Group, Inc.)

Duran, Joe (Joseph J.)
The money code : improve your entire financial life right now /
Joe John Duran. — 1st ed.

p. ; cm.

"... a modern tale of one person's journey to uncover the five secrets to living his one best financial life." — Publisher's description.

ISBN: 978-1-60832-435-4

1. Finance, Personal. I. Title.

HG179 .D87 2013

332.024   2012947912

For ordering information or special discounts for bulk purchases, please contact Greenleaf Book Group, LLC at P.O. Box 91869, Austin, TX 78709, telephone 512.891.6100

Part of the Tree Neutral® program, which offsets the number of trees consumed in the production and printing of this book by taking proactive steps, such as planting trees in direct proportion to the number of trees used: TreeNeutral.com

TreeNeutral®

Printed in the United States of America on acid-free paper

12 13 14 15 16 10 9 8 7 6 5 4 3 2 1

First Edition

This book is dedicated to the brilliant, inspirational, and strong women who have guided me throughout my life—from my tough-as-nails mother and big-hearted sisters to my three darling daughters: Charlotte, Juliette, and Samantha, who are such wonderful young ladies and who give my life richness and meaning. But most importantly, this book is dedicated to the one woman who has always believed in me, held me up, and challenged me to do good in this world—my soul mate and muse, my home, and my star for the past quarter of a century: Jennifer. I love you and appreciate you for helping me grow every day.

ACKNOWLEDGMENTS

Writing this third book has been one of the most pleasurable and exciting experiences of my life because of the work of Lawrence Ineno, who helped to craft, refine, and write this story with me for the past year. His unwavering passion and belief in the underlying premise and his desire to constantly improve on what we have done helped to create something we are both really proud of. Lawrence's care, talent, and gentle yet insightful guidance are the single biggest reason this book was completed.

I also would like to thank Carl Richards, author of The Behavior Gap, *for his brilliant graphics and insights. We are kindred spirits in our desire to help people make better decisions.*

Lastly, I need to acknowledge the incredibly talented individuals I work with, who really provided all the knowledge in this book and who pour their hearts and minds into improving the lives of thousands of people around the country every single day—helping to guide, inform, and counsel individuals and their families about their entire financial life. I am so proud to be a part of your lives and to play a small part in everything you do to improve an industry that has for too long cared more about itself than the people it serves. You are an inspiration.

TABLE OF CONTENTS

A VOYAGE OF DISCOVERY

At 34 years old, I experienced the pinnacle of the American dream. My business partners and I had successfully sold our investment firm to General Electric, which freed me to do whatever I wanted.

Prior to reaching this career milestone, I had always assumed that a big payday like this would signal an end to my perpetual fear of failure. But being free to do whatever I wanted gave me no sense of freedom at all. In fact, what should have been a time of relief and joy instead filled me with uncertainty about the future. To make matters worse, I felt no real comfort about my family's financial situation. So rather than take time to enjoy life with my amazing wife and darling daughters and celebrate my professional accomplishment, I immediately threw myself back into work.

As I reflect on my past, I recognize something that was true for me and for many of the folks I've helped throughout my career: *Money was enslaving me rather than giving me genuine freedom.*

Thankfully, my perspective about money has evolved. For change to occur, however, I had to take an honest look at what was keeping me from genuine personal and financial freedom. This reality check has opened up new possibilities that would have otherwise gone unnoticed. It has also completely altered the way I make financial decisions and how I express—to those whom I cherish—what I care about most.

AN OBJECTIVE PERSPECTIVE WILL GIVE YOU CLARITY

Ideally, making decisions about money would be a solely intellectual exercise. But I have come to know—as both an individual and a financial professional—that decisions about money are almost always emotional ones, too. And our personal histories and perspectives will affect not just how we make decisions but also their quality.

In order to experience financial success, we must distinguish our emotional motivation from our logical, or "brain," motivation. Also, having an open and sincere approach to discussing money issues is crucial to maintaining a unified partnership with others.

To solve this challenge that we all face, I assembled a team of brilliant, forward-thinking professionals. Together we developed a simple, yet profoundly precise, way to bridge the gap between what individuals *say they want* and what they're *actually doing*. The latter is often what prevents people from living their one best financial life. This book will show you our breakthrough approach, which is shaking up the world of financial thinking.

When it comes to your finances, accepting your reality and feelings—warts and all—is the first step toward creating real change. And be assured that if you've ever found yourself confused, fearful, frozen in indecision, in conflict with those you love, or feeling any combination of the preceding, you're in good company.

I can't guarantee that our approach will result in your financial success. But I can say with complete confidence that the methods presented in this book have dramatically improved the financial lives of a wide range of people across the U.S., and I have no doubt that you'll find this to be an exciting and personally enlightening voyage.

In the end, my greatest hope is that you'll realize genuine financial freedom and peace of mind beyond what you may have thought possible. So let's get started!

CHAPTER 1
The Problem with Money

Money, by itself, is good for very little. These words may seem odd coming from someone whose career has been rooted in the financial world. But I've learned that our personal views and how we interact with money are what give the almighty dollar the immense power to create happiness or cause suffering.

From the moment we can understand language, we're presented with conflicting views about money. On one hand, it makes the world go 'round, and on the other, it's the root of all evil. If we love money, we're greedy; if we're indifferent to it, we're irresponsible; and if we hate it, we're card-carrying communist party members.

The truth is, most of us were raised without really talking about money or learning how to make decisions involving it. As a result, figuring out what money means to each of us often seems like an impossible task. And more importantly, our uncertainty has forced many of us to find our own way, which has most likely led us to make many mistakes throughout our lives.

MONEY: WHAT'S IT GOOD FOR?

Here's the simple truth about money—it can really only help you do three things in your life:

1. **Avoid pain**—by protecting you and helping you to take care of what you're afraid might cause pain in the future

2. **Feel good**—by getting you the things that provide you with happiness and satisfaction
3. **Take care of the ones you love**—by meeting your obligations to family, community, and society at large

So how do you unravel what money means to you in order to improve your financial life?

First, you need a desire to create lasting change. Second, you need a guide. The fact that you're reading these words points to your motivation to bring about better outcomes, and as far as guidance is concerned, the goal of this book is to provide the lasting financial solutions you've been looking for.

REALIZING THE AMERICAN DREAM, VERSION 2.0

As a whole, the financial services industry is accustomed to talking about money in mathematical terms. No doubt this has improved the lives of people across the country. But the science of numbers and quantity has been insufficient on its own.

In fact, survey after survey reinforces the same fact: People feel that they are not well trained when it comes to making financial decisions. In addition, many feel that the only winners are the big institutions selling investment solutions, and they're convinced that they're not doing as well as others when it comes to money and investing.

As a financial professional, I have firsthand experience with the broad discontent that many people have. Innumerable individuals and families express the following frustrations:

- *I don't really have control over my financial life.*
- *It feels as though I never have enough money.*
- *I wish I could have a simpler financial life.*
- *Making big financial decisions makes me nervous.*
- *I keep making the same investment mistakes.*
- *I'm sick of arguing about money with those closest to me.*

Amazingly, many of these individuals are wealthy and have worked with some type of financial adviser for years.

TIME TO GET HONEST ABOUT MONEY

The core of this book lies in the Money Code, which comprises 5 Money Secrets. The five secrets will provide insights into your decision making and help you evaluate how you think and feel about money and assess the way you make financial decisions. These simple, eternal truths have moved countless individuals and families away from the belief that finance is a strictly intellectual endeavor. More importantly, these five uncompromising truths have put people just like you in the driver's seat of their financial lives, which has given them genuine, lasting control over their money.

The 5 Money Secrets are as follows:

1. Your life will be filled with tough choices.
2. Your entire life is determined by how you make decisions.
3. Your biases will affect every decision you make.
4. You will be distracted by things that really don't matter.
5. You must have a good process to make good decisions.

Our feelings and beliefs about money are highly personal. That's why, in the next chapters, you'll see how the 5 Money Secrets work through the eyes of Jack, a fictional character whose encounter with a benevolent friend dramatically changes how he makes decisions about money. Through Jack's example, you'll understand how the Money Code can play a key role in improving your financial life. In addition, you'll receive a checklist that you can use whenever you're faced with an important financial decision, and you'll discover how to apply the checklist to yourself as well as someone you care about.

This book isn't intended to change your feelings or thoughts about money. Rather, it's meant to help you understand yourself and those around you as well as to provide you with a road map for making sound financial decisions. In the end, you only have one financial life, so why not make the most of it?

CHAPTER 2

The Journey of a Lifetime

"*Ever since we separated*, it's been hard for me to make decisions, especially when it comes to money," Jack said.

"I'm really surprised to hear that because I never thought you worried about money," said Claudia, Jack's younger sister. She was at his house visiting her young niece, who was napping upstairs.

"I didn't, and that's probably one of the biggest reasons behind our split—Olivia got fed up with my lack of discipline when it came to our finances," he said.

Throughout their marriage, Olivia constantly complained about how Jack spent too much and didn't plan enough about saving for the future. At the same time, he dreaded having financial discussions, which would usually become deeply frustrating for both of them. Now the small business owner found himself 40 years old and with a shrunken nest egg, thanks to the separation and a series of bad investment decisions. He knew that from this point on, reaching his financial goals would require him to pay more attention to his spending habits.

"The breakup has really hit me hard. I'm constantly second-guessing myself whenever I have to make decisions—even small ones," Jack confessed. A few weeks ago, he agreed to take a trip with his best friend. He now wondered if he should have said yes so soon. Despite his doubt, however, one thing was for sure: The knot in his stomach was all too familiar.

"You've been talking about visiting Machu Picchu since long before you two separated. So why the worry all of a sudden?" asked Claudia.

Jack couldn't pinpoint the source of his concern. Perhaps he was pre-occupied with what Olivia would think about the trip. But at the same time, he really needed to get away in order to gain insight into himself and what had gone wrong in his marriage.

"This is going to sound horrible, but I partly blame Mom and Dad for a lot of the confusion I'm having these days," he said.

"What do you mean?"

"So much of my recent stress boils down to feeling lost when it comes to money," Jack replied. "They never talked to us about it. In fact, the only time I remember hearing about money was when they'd argue. Don't get me wrong, I know that they were pretty amazing parents. But the older I get, the more I'm seeing that for all they taught us, they left us completely unprepared in one crucial way."

He thought about his father, who worried about money incessantly when they were young and still did. Jack vowed never to do the same. Lately, however, his anxieties mirrored his dad's. "Mom and Dad never taught us how to make good financial decisions or even how to think about money and its role in our lives," he said.

Now that he was a parent, Jack felt responsible for teaching his young daughter to make better choices than he did. But he was clueless about how to start.

JACK AND CLAUDIA FIND COMMON GROUND

Claudia considered Jack's observation. "Between the two of us, I always felt like I was the only one who was completely lost when it came to money. Remember the mess I was in a few years ago?" Back then, Claudia's anxieties had reached a tipping point: She was buried under student loans and credit card debt and felt as though there was no way out.

Jack responded, "I remember Mom and Dad telling me that they were worried about you. They even asked me to talk to you. But I didn't want it to seem like your big brother was interfering, so I left it up to you to reach out."

"I nearly asked you for help," Claudia said. "But at the moment when I was barely treading water, someone tossed me a lifesaver, and things haven't been the same since." Claudia shared that she'd met with a guide who had changed her financial life forever. He was called the Alchemist.

"What's up with the name?"

"He has a real one. But he goes by the Alchemist, and I think now's the perfect time for you to meet him," she said.

Jack wasn't sure what was so perfect about the timing. "Can you tell me a little more about this guy first?" he asked.

"The short answer is no. But before I explain why, let me ask you this: Since that time five years ago when everyone was so worried about my future, have you noticed a change in me?" she asked.

Jack reflected on the financial milestones that his sister had reached during the past few years: She took a trip to celebrate paying off her student loans and credit card debt, and she bought a two-bedroom condominium. He also noticed that she seemed happier and more focused and at ease.

"So if I were to say that I had the Alchemist to thank for the major turnaround in my life, would you believe me?" she asked.

"Of course I would. But how does that help me?"

"Because the Alchemist's advice applies to anyone who's ready," she answered.

"How can you be sure about that?" he asked.

"He taught me that for everything we're conditioned to think about money—what it can and can't do, how it's good, how it's evil, how it corrupts, and countless other magical powers we attribute to it—it can really only do three things: help protect us from pain, help us do the things that make us happy, and help us look after the people we love. That's it—everything else is nonessential," she said. "But more importantly, if we don't take control and apply awareness to our thinking, money has the power to take over our lives."

Claudia's explanation intuitively made sense to Jack. He also appreciated that his younger sister was looking out for him. So despite his skepticism, he decided he'd take her up on the offer. Claudia pulled a business card out of her wallet and handed it to him.

It was worn around the edges and had obviously been in Claudia's wallet for a long time.

"No first and last name, not even an email address?" Jack asked. He then flipped over the card.

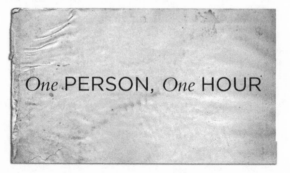

"What the heck does that mean?" asked Jack.

"That's another thing I didn't tell you. He'll change your life in 60 minutes, but you'll need to do a little work before you meet with him. And one more thing—please don't share the card with anyone until you've had your face-to-face meeting with him," said Claudia.

"Alright, this is getting a little weird," he said.

"Not at all. It just has to do with keeping a promise I made."

"What kind of promise?" Jack asked.

"That I'd keep the card."

"Then are you sure you want to part with it? I can just jot down the number."

Claudia replied, "No, it's yours. In fact, it was meant for you, and you'll find out why later. Besides, I'm happy to finally be teaching *you* something. Just be sure to tell the Alchemist that I gave you his card when you call."

Although Jack wouldn't admit it to his little sister, his curiosity had been piqued. If nothing else, he was fascinated to find out who had brainwashed her so successfully.

CHAPTER 3
The Background Check

After Claudia left, Jack went to his home office, hopped online, and searched "alchemist." With over 14,000,000 results, he knew it would be impossible to find out more about his sister's mentor. On Wikipedia, however, he did find the following:

"The defining goal of alchemy is often given as the transmutation of common metals into gold."

Jack remembered a book he'd read years ago about an alchemist who learned to create wealth from the wind. A series of doubts crossed his mind: Did his sister line him up for a get-rich-quick scheme or a pyramid sales ploy? Or worse, some weird religious cult? But his hesitation subsided when he reminded himself that it was just one phone call. What was there to be afraid of? After all, he could always end the conversation. He dialed the number on the card. Voicemail picked up:

You've reached the Alchemist. Please leave your name and number, and be sure to state who gave you my card.

Moments after leaving a short message, Jack received a text:

I'll call you in five minutes.

The quick response surprised him, and the nervous feeling inside made him wonder whether this was worth all the effort over a silly trip to Peru.

THE FIRST CONVERSATION

Exactly five minutes later, the Alchemist's phone number glowed on Jack's screen. His blood pressure surged as he debated whether or not to answer. He counted: one ring, two, and then three. Finally on the fourth—the one right before voicemail would pick up—he hit the "Answer Call" button.

"Hello?"

"Hi, Jack. It's the Alchemist," the man of mystery said.

"Thanks for your call," Jack said. He decided to be polite rather than express his cynicism over the entire thing.

"I'm glad that Claudia suggested you reach out to me. It's probably been five years since I last spoke with her. How's she doing these days?" he asked.

"Doing well. You may know this already—Claudia's my younger sister," Jack said.

"So I'm speaking to a sibling? Well, you're a lucky brother. I respect Claudia immensely. Almost as much as she respects and cares for you," he said.

The Alchemist's response took him aback. First off, Jack had assumed that his sister had been in regular contact with the Alchemist. So if the two hadn't spoken in half a decade, and he wasn't aware that Jack existed, how did the Alchemist know that Claudia respected him? He guessed it was a canned response that he used for everyone.

"I bet you're wondering how I know that your sister respects you," said the Alchemist.

"Since you didn't know who I was until now, the thought did cross my mind," Jack said. He was slightly disarmed by how the Alchemist was able to navigate a conversation with a stranger with such ease.

"I'll sum it up with this: One person, one hour," he said.

"Hey, that's from your card! What exactly does that mean?" Jack asked.

"This may come as a surprise, but I've only met Claudia once. Although our meeting only lasted an hour, those 60 minutes changed her life forever," he said.

"How's that possible?" Jack asked.

"You'd be surprised by how much you can accomplish when you have a disciplined process. I can't go into detail about it right now, but I promise you'll understand later."

The Alchemist added that after their meeting, he told Claudia to keep his business card and to give it to one other person. That individual needed to be somebody she cared for deeply—a person who would benefit most from the one hour.

"So I'm the one person," said Jack. He thought of all the people whom Claudia could have given the business card to, but instead it had remained in her wallet for five years. Suddenly the call took on greater significance.

"It also explains how I know she respects and cares for you so much. Please forgive me if I sound impolite, but before we move on, I need some basic information from you to see if we're a good fit," he said.

"A good fit?" Jack asked. He thought it presumptuous for the Alchemist to assume that Jack was even interested.

"Are you tired of the way you're making financial decisions?" the Alchemist asked.

"Well…kind of," Jack said. He wasn't sure where the question was headed, which made him uneasy.

"Is that a yes or a no?" the Alchemist asked.

"Uh, I guess I'd say yes," Jack answered reluctantly, feeling confronted.

"So what you're telling me is that the way you're making decisions is broken," said the Alchemist.

The subject of making decisions struck a nerve. Since his separation from Olivia, Jack constantly doubted his judgment, especially when it came to his finances.

"Look, I really appreciate your time, but your questions are making me uncomfortable. I only contacted you because I was planning a trip to Peru, and Claudia told me to give you a call."

"Before you give up on our talk, I'd like you to answer four simple yes-or-no questions," the Alchemist said. "I call them the 'Four Honest Questions About Your Financial Wellness.' All I ask is that you answer them as truthfully as possible."

The request seemed painless enough, so Jack agreed. The Alchemist asked him the following:

THE FOUR HONEST QUESTIONS ABOUT YOUR FINANCIAL WELLNESS

1. Do you avoid making decisions about money?
2. Do you feel as though you're missing something in your financial life?
3. Have you made money decisions you've regretted and then repeated the same mistakes?
4. Does talking about money with the people you love make you feel uncomfortable?

The questions summed up Jack's biggest struggles with money—things he'd never been able to articulate on his own.

"Yes, I avoid making decisions about money. Yes, I feel uncomfortable with my financial life. To be honest, I've never felt genuine peace of mind when it comes to money. Yes, I make the same mistakes over and over. And yes, talking about money makes me uncomfortable—in fact, I was just complaining to my sister about that last one," Jack said. His confession provided immediate relief.

"Are you currently working with a financial adviser, insurance broker, estate planning lawyer, CPA, or any combination of them?" the Alchemist asked.

"I have a financial adviser at a big firm who's also a friend. I have an accountant and an insurance broker, too."

"So despite paying experts your hard-earned dollars to guide you, you still have a dysfunctional relationship with money. This leads me to conclude that your current anxieties are bigger than the one issue you might be confronting right now, wouldn't you say?" the Alchemist asked.

"I kind of get your point, but I'm still not exactly sure what you mean," Jack said. "I'm really only calling because I feel anxious about whether I can afford to take a trip that I've dreamed about for years."

NEW APPROACHES TO OLD PROBLEMS

The Alchemist explained that Jack's current dilemma was rooted in patterns and behaviors that ran far deeper than the trip itself. He was, in fact, being presented with two options: He could address the vacation as an isolated situation, which would be akin to covering a serious wound with a tiny Band-Aid, or he could treat the real challenge head-on, which might be more painful at first, but it would generate a far healthier and longer-lasting outcome that could improve his entire life forever.

"The choice is yours," said the Alchemist.

The Alchemist's insight disarmed Jack. How was this stranger able to articulate his current state with such precision?

The Alchemist continued, "If I provided a way to forever change how you thought and made decisions about money through a proven formula that has improved the lives of a select few, like your sister, would you be interested? But before you answer, I'll add that in order for it to work, you must agree with the 'Two Eternal Truths About Decision Making.'"

"What are they?" Jack asked.

The Alchemist explained the following:

THE TWO ETERNAL TRUTHS
ABOUT DECISION MAKING

1. Lack of clarity and understanding of yourself and the situation at hand will lead to poor decisions.

2. Creating lasting change requires you to be honest with yourself and to be disciplined and persistent.

Jack, a skeptic by nature, couldn't believe that the same person he'd been ready to hang up on had now convinced him that his financial life up to this point had been completely misguided. To his surprise, he found himself immediately acknowledging the validity of the "Two Eternal Truths About Decision Making."

"You're right," Jack said. "Without a clear and truthful assessment of myself and the situation I'm facing, it's impossible to make good, informed decisions throughout my life."

"Glad to hear it. I'm sure you have lots of other questions. Unfortunately, my time is limited. That's actually why I didn't pick up right away when you called. I had to check my calendar in order to schedule a meeting with you. How's the Monday after next at 7:00 p.m.?"

That Monday would be Jack's birthday. The Alchemist's seeming sixth sense as well as the rapid pace of the discussion disoriented him. Before he could disclose the possible schedule conflict, the Alchemist pushed the conversation forward.

"Agreed? Great. I'll send you directions for where we'll meet. But before I do that, I have one more requirement," the Alchemist said.

"What is it?" asked Jack.

THE 5 SECRETS TO BREAKING THE MONEY CODE

The Alchemist shared that he would provide Jack with a username and password for a private website where he would learn about the Money Code.

"Prior to our face-to-face meeting, you're going to learn the 5 Money Secrets that make up the Money Code. They are as follows:

1. Your life will be filled with tough choices.
2. Your entire life is determined by how you make decisions.
3. Your biases will affect every decision you make.
4. You will be distracted by things that really don't matter.
5. You must have a good process to make good decisions.

"With the exception of the first lesson, which is an overview of the 5 Money Secrets, there will be a space at the end of each lesson for you to summarize what you have learned. I ask that you write down, in simple terms, what the lesson taught you. Once you've completed the assignment, you'll have another lesson waiting for you online. Don't worry about remembering my directions—they'll be repeated on the website," he said.

The Alchemist added that the Money Code came from a lifetime of experience helping people from a wide range of backgrounds. Jack didn't have to read the lessons six days in a row. He just needed to complete all six of them by the time they met in two weeks. "The reason I give you a lesson at a time is because they build on each other, so it's important not to skip any. And by trickling them out, you'll be able to think more deeply about these seemingly simple, yet life-changing, ideas," he said.

"How long do you think each lesson will take?" Jack asked. He was a busy entrepreneur and was concerned about the time commitment.

"Not long. Probably around 20 minutes of actual reading—longer if you think very hard about what each lesson means to you. I hope that you'll invest time in contemplating and internalizing the implications of each one before you write your summary," the Alchemist said.

Between his laptop, smartphone, and tablet, Jack knew that he could read the lessons and complete the exercises within two weeks. "I know you have to go, but may I ask one last question?" he asked.

"Sure, what is it?"

"Why the name?" Jack asked.

"An alchemist transforms lead into gold. In that respect, I'm no alchemist. But I do dramatically change people's perspectives, and I like to think I help people make something special and valuable from nothing. I teach people like you that you can have anything you want in this world, but in order to get it, you must remove multiple barriers. I hope that when we meet, we'll take away the emotional roadblocks that keep you from attaining genuine peace of mind when making financial decisions," he said.

"I look forward to it," Jack said.

The Alchemist provided Jack with the information to access the Money Code website.

"See you in two weeks," said the Alchemist.

CHAPTER 4
Jack Enters the Alchemist's Website

"It's going to be another sleepless night," Jack told himself as he shifted his body—once again—in his bed. Unlike his previous bouts of insomnia, however, it wasn't the trip to Machu Picchu that would keep him up tonight. Rather, it had to do with the talk that took place between the Alchemist and him a few hours ago. During their ten-minute conversation, Jack was presented with ideas that challenged his perspective and the way he had lived his entire financial life.

Although he planned to begin his assignment the next day, he knew that sleep would probably elude him. So he decided to get an early start on the reading.

Jack entered his home office, plopped himself in front of the computer, and woke it from sleep. When he input the address, a simple login window appeared. He entered the information he had jotted down earlier:

---[MONEY CODE]---
LOGIN

Username | Jack
Password | ********

ENTER

He clicked "enter," and his information was accepted. He then read the following page:

HELLO, JACK!

You've arrived at the Money Code website.

As I shared with you when we spoke, I'll provide you with a total of six lessons, presented one at a time. You can only read one a day. Please complete all six before we meet.

Let's get started!

Best regards, The Alchemist

Jack then read the following:

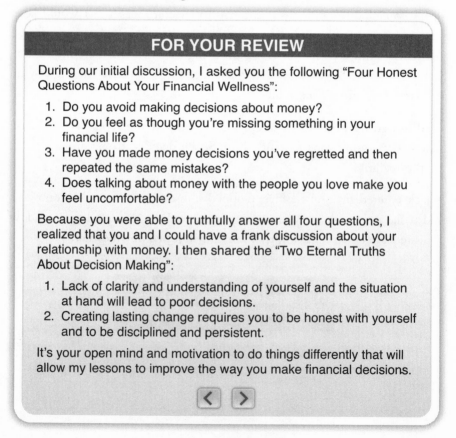

FOR YOUR REVIEW

During our initial discussion, I asked you the following "Four Honest Questions About Your Financial Wellness":

1. Do you avoid making decisions about money?
2. Do you feel as though you're missing something in your financial life?
3. Have you made money decisions you've regretted and then repeated the same mistakes?
4. Does talking about money with the people you love make you feel uncomfortable?

Because you were able to truthfully answer all four questions, I realized that you and I could have a frank discussion about your relationship with money. I then shared the "Two Eternal Truths About Decision Making":

1. Lack of clarity and understanding of yourself and the situation at hand will lead to poor decisions.
2. Creating lasting change requires you to be honest with yourself and to be disciplined and persistent.

It's your open mind and motivation to do things differently that will allow my lessons to improve the way you make financial decisions.

Once Jack finished reading the overview, he clicked the "next" arrow. The following appeared:

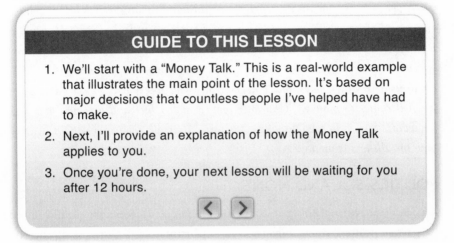

Jack clicked the "next" arrow. The first page of his inaugural assignment appeared. He propped himself up in his chair, took a sip from the bottle of water that was sitting on his desk, and plunged into the first lesson that the Alchemist had prepared for him.

JACK READS AN OVERVIEW OF THE MONEY SECRETS

$ MONEY TALK: THE BIG DECISION

"Rod, we really need to talk about this—we just can't keep putting it off," Charlotte said. She had been trying to get her husband to discuss their son's college tuition for months, but she could never find the right time. She'd tried after work, waited until the weekend, and even spoiled a good dinner when she tried talking about it over a glass of wine at a restaurant. It never seemed as though the timing was right. Whenever she brought it up, Rod's face would flush, and he'd grumble about not wanting to talk about it.

As expected, he let out a sigh and looked annoyed at the mention of another money discussion, even though they both knew that college tuition loomed on the horizon. Charlotte persisted, "Look, it's no easier for me, but we both need to be able to have a conversation about this stuff without you ignoring me or getting mad."

Rod looked at his wife and could see that he wouldn't be able to blow her off this time, so he braced himself for another disagreement. It seemed as though whenever money came up, one of them would wind up annoyed, while the other one got what he or she wanted but not without a great deal of struggle. Finally Rod spoke up. "Honey, I know it's important for us to talk about it, but I really don't want to fight. Isn't there a better way for us to get through this? We do so well in other ways, but I never really feel like we're on the same page when it comes to money." Charlotte looked at her husband and was at a loss for words. She didn't know where to start. After all, who ever taught anyone how to talk about money?

POLITICS, SEX, AND MONEY

We've all grown up being told about the three subjects that should never be part of polite dinner conversation. Unfortunately, not discussing the last one—money—has led many Americans to financial frustrations and concerns that are seldom addressed.

We might not like thinking about it, we might not like discussing it, and we might not like having to make decisions about it, but there's no escaping the fact that money affects every aspect of our lives. So isn't it about time we started talking candidly about it? The lessons I've created for you are about having an open discussion about money—one that you should have with yourself as well as with the people you love.

IT'S NEVER ABOUT THE MONEY. IT'S ALWAYS ABOUT HOW WE FEEL ABOUT OUR MONEY.

Americans love to measure and track. From our cholesterol levels to the latest results of presidential polls, we are obsessed with statistics. When it comes to personal finances, we maintain a similar emphasis on facts. Our financial lives are often reduced to a series of stale questions such as, "What are our assets and liabilities?" "How much do we have in our retirement accounts?" and "How much are we making on our money?"

This singular emphasis on number crunching has trained us to view our financial lives as an intellectual endeavor, effectively stripping the "personal" from "personal finance." Although we can measure all we want, almost every major financial decision we make is based on emotions.

TIME FOR A CHANGE

Unfortunately, fact-based approaches to money have yielded subpar results for most of us. In countless surveys, when asked about the state of their finances, respondents answered with a resounding "dissatisfied." And if you thought it was only those who are struggling to get by who feel this way, you'd be mistaken. Having money—even lots of it—doesn't guarantee satisfaction or peace of mind. I can personally attest to that. Growing up, my parents often struggled to make ends meet. I later became a successful entrepreneur. Despite the financial accomplishments of adulthood, past fears and insecurities persisted and haunted my entire life.

We are all bound together by this one truth: *No major financial decision gets made without our emotions playing a starring role.* So why is it that when it comes to money, we overemphasize the data while neglecting our subjective experiences and perspectives? I believe that this is because focusing on facts and figures is safe. Meanwhile, few people have learned how to evaluate and discuss what really matters to them about their money. In addition, the evolution of the financial services industry holds some answers.

A SHORT (VERY SHORT) HISTORY OF U.S. INVESTING

At the turn of the last century, a wave of economic prosperity extended across the United States. As a result, an unprecedented number of individuals had savings in excess of their living expenses. Meanwhile, the stock and bond markets were growing in both size and complexity.

Those who had cash to invest turned to brokers whose job was to put their clients' money into the stock and bond markets. These advisers—nearly all male—also served as consultants. They made the complex language of Wall Street accessible to the masses. And the more complicated the industry became, the more the public had to rely on so-called experts for help. Since then, most financial professionals have viewed it as their responsibility to take complete charge of their clients' financial lives.

Therefore, many professionals in the financial services industry are technicians who love facts and figures. They have brought a specialized language and perspective to the way we discuss money. The problem is that almost every one of our big financial decisions involves emotions, which aren't something that a lot of technically minded experts want to talk about!

Fast-forward to the present. Many individuals aren't satisfied with the way they deal with their own money but can't explain why. Their lack of clarity and direction often results in poor decisions with even worse outcomes. Howard Marks, a highly respected institutional investor, puts it best. He says that every financial decision is driven by one of two fears:

- **Fear of missing opportunities**
- **Fear of losing money**

Sometimes people are conscious that their motivations are based on fears or desires. For instance, a wary investor may say, "I'm feeling scared, and I need to do what's best to protect my investments."

Often, however, fear and desire play stealthier roles. "I've heard everyone is making money in gold, so I'd better buy some," another investor may say.

In either case, failing to recognize what is driving our decisions is hazardous to our financial health. The following recent examples of historical significance illustrate the dangers of not understanding the two fears and how they cloud our judgment.

1999 TECH BUBBLE: FEAR OF MISSING OPPORTUNITIES

The investing masses saw endless opportunity in what became known as the Information Revolution. From Pets.com (epic failure) to Amazon (massive success), many viewed tech stocks as providing unprecedented opportunities for growth. The media fueled the hype by regularly reporting about Silicon Valley start-ups that turned recent college grads and even high school dropouts into instant millionaires. Although there was no question that most of these new high-tech stocks were overpriced, investors ignored the data. Millions of Americans invested in them because they didn't want to miss the opportunity of a lifetime.

The dot.com boom went bust, and some investors lost their entire savings as a result. And more recently, the same fear of missing opportunities sent home prices into a bubble. The housing market crashed at the end of the last decade, and we're still paying the price.

2008 STOCK MARKET COLLAPSE AND SUBSEQUENT RECOVERY: FEAR OF LOSING MONEY

The stock market plummeted, and droves of investors reacted by selling their investments. After seeing their portfolios' values nosedive, individuals became skittish about stocks. Despite their trepidation, the stock market's value doubled over the next few years. Only then did these reluctant investors consider reentering the stock market. Sadly, their waiting resulted in missed opportunities to invest at incredibly low prices.

5 MONEY SECRETS: INSPIRING NEW WAYS TO THINK ABOUT YOUR MONEY

One of the main reasons you and I are working together is that you're tired of being driven by fears and desires. Throughout this lesson, I've pointed out that identifying finance as a strictly intellectual endeavor has not served your needs. My goal is to lead you toward living your one best financial life.

Although what money alone can do is limited, its power to create happiness or cause suffering is immense. The following 5 Money Secrets provide a powerful way to guide your decision making so that you can take genuine control of your financial life.

1. Your life will be filled with tough choices.
2. Your entire life is determined by how you make decisions.
3. Your biases will affect every decision you make.
4. You will be distracted by things that really don't matter.
5. You must have a good process to make good decisions.

Jack arrived at the last page of the Alchemist's lesson.

THE WRAP-UP

GREAT JOB, JACK!

You've reached the end of your first lesson. Over the next five, I'll describe each Money Secret. Then I'll provide further insight into how each one deeply influences how you make financial decisions.

Your next lesson will be waiting for you 12 hours from the moment you log out of my website.

Best regards, The Alchemist

Jack reflected on what he had just read. He realized that anxieties about money had not only driven his own financial decisions but, based on the historical events that the Alchemist described, those of entire nations. "At least I'm in good company when it comes to my misunderstandings and fears," he thought to himself.

Although he had just embarked on his journey with the Alchemist, Jack already felt a sense of ease—a confidence that came from seeing that in less than 24 hours, he had, for the first time, noticed a genuine awareness with regard to his relationship with money.

Jack rubbed his weary eyes, no longer feeling the anxiety that kept him up. He logged out of the Alchemist's website, returned to bed, and fell asleep.

CHAPTER 5
Jack's Second Lesson

Jack sat at his desk after a long workday. Over 12 hours had passed since he had read the Alchemist's first lesson. He logged on to the Alchemist's website.

HELLO, JACK!

Welcome back. I hope you enjoyed the introductory lesson.

Now let's get started on the first Money Secret!

Best regards, The Alchemist

< >

GUIDE TO THIS LESSON

1. After you learn about Money Secret 1, you'll read a "Money Talk."

2. Toward the end of this lesson, you'll read a section called "Questions to Ask Yourself." Here, I present food for thought regarding the Money Talk.

3. In the "What the Money Secret Means to You" section, I've provided you with space to write a brief summary of the lesson. Once you submit it, I'll review it within 12 hours.

Jack took a sip from his coffee mug. He looked forward to what he'd learn today.

MONEY SECRET 1:
YOUR LIFE WILL BE FILLED WITH TOUGH CHOICES.

YOU WANT IT ALL

Part of consumer culture is that from early on, we're taught to think big. Every American can dream of owning a nicer car. We drool over bigger TVs. We vow to take more vacations. We fantasize about fancier shoes and jewelry. With a combination of envy and disdain, we read stories of the super rich with their mega mansions and private jets.

Sometimes it's a blessing; other times, it's a curse. In either case, we humans have a limitless ability to dream bigger and to always elevate our aspirations. This is true whether you're a schoolteacher struggling to make ends meet or you're a billionaire, like Bill Gates, debating how to improve the lives of as many impoverished people as possible—and, for the more self-interested super rich, how big a yacht they can afford!

At some point, however, you must acknowledge the reality of your circumstances. Usually, you *can't* have it all. So you have to make choices. Neglecting to make tradeoffs can lead to credit card debt, a persistent inferiority complex, and constant financial pressure. The bottom line is that *each of us has one ideal financial life that we envision, but we seldom have enough resources to live it the way we'd like.* To reach your fullest potential requires you to identify the intersection between two elements:

- **Your current dreams and goals**
- **Your finite resources**

Your resources include not just the money and assets you have today, but also your ability to generate income in the future. Attaining balance is difficult because most of us dream about having more than we can currently afford. Therefore, to find balance, you must continually ask yourself, "What am I willing to accept and have with my current resources?" The question becomes even more challenging when you share your life with someone you love.

YOUR EVER-CHANGING FINANCIAL LIFE

Your financial goals and resources are seldom in sync, and to complicate things even more, *they are constantly changing.* For example, when you started your first job, you may have hoped for a steady income and to one day live in a nicer place. After you met your first love, your hopes and dreams changed in order to include another person. The day you stayed in a more luxurious hotel, you added another must-have to your list of things you'd like to enjoy more frequently. These examples illustrate that at any given moment, you can see or feel something that inspires you to reach for more.

Think about all of the events, large and small, that immediately change your hopes and dreams the minute they occur:

- You graduate from college.
- You get married.
- You see the newest BMW.
- You start your own company.
- Your child is born.
- You go to an orphanage and see children in need.
- You take a trip to Italy.

- You're in a dreadful car accident.
- Your parents fall ill.

The list of things that change your perspective and give you a different set of hopes and dreams is literally endless. These changes take place through-out your lifetime.

In addition, your resources are always in flux. And things completely out of your control often drive them. Here's a short list:

- You lose your job.
- You get a promotion.
- You inherit some money.
- Taxes go up.
- The dollar goes down.
- Inflation increases.
- Social security payments decline.

Every time your resources change, the potential financial life you can lead changes as well. So being satisfied with your financial life requires you to have a clear way to make tradeoffs and to understand the goals and dreams you're will-ing to adjust if you have to. These two factors—making tradeoffs and modifying your dreams—are also essential to attaining a genuine sense of control.

$ MONEY TALK: THE HOME REMODEL

Once the meeting with the architect wrapped up, Kathleen couldn't wait to share the latest renovation plans with her husband. The new kitchen would include a Sub-Zero refrigerator, the master bedroom would have his-and-hers walk-in closets, the backyard would be gutted to make room for an infinity pool, and more.

The moment Ken arrived home that evening, Kathleen greeted him with a heart-felt hug. They sat down and reviewed the architect's sketches. "Can you believe how great it looks?" she exclaimed.

"Yeah, but what's the bottom line?" Ken asked.

"$250,000," Kathleen answered. His audible exhale signaled his concern, and she knew it. "Honey, don't worry. We're both doing great at work, we've got plenty of equity in the house, and the remodel will make it worth even more," she said. Part of him wanted to bring up why this might not be a good idea: Their entire rainy day fund would most likely go toward the remodel, they probably wouldn't be able to contribute to their retirement and children's college funds, and the renovation could take longer and cost more than they anticipated. He knew, however, that sharing his concerns would probably lead to an argument. "At the end of the day, is it worth taking on so much risk?" he wondered to himself.

THINKING THROUGH THEIR CIRCUMSTANCES

Kathleen and Ken's Goals and Dreams: As the home renovation progressed, the project became more and more elaborate. Although the remodel's cost was high, the couple believed that it would be a good long-term investment and that it would enrich their lives. Meanwhile, they still wanted to give their children a fantastic education and fund a comfortable retirement.

The Couple's Resources: They were both earning solid incomes, and their home's equity had increased. But the remodel would deplete their savings, including their emergency fund. It would also concentrate all of their financial resources into their home, which meant that they wouldn't be able to contribute to their retirement plans or their children's college savings.

The Challenge: Ken and Kathleen didn't have complete information. For instance, they had no constructive way to evaluate how much they could really afford to spend on the remodel. In other words, they lacked a system that would ensure that they didn't risk everything else that mattered to them, such as maintaining a safety net to cover emergencies or educating their children through college. In addition, they couldn't say with certainty that their home's value would continue to increase, and they didn't know whether their incomes would keep growing. Lastly, Ken had been supportive of the remodel, but he was feeling anxiety over the mounting drawbacks. Unfortunately, he didn't know how to effectively communicate his concerns.

The Consequences: They had no margin of error in their financial lives if they went ahead with their dream project as designed. In addition, the couple didn't have a clear decision-making process that would help them prioritize all of their goals. The current remodel was one example of many in which either Kathleen or Ken would always feel excluded and frustrated. The absence of a clear decision-making process would also have serious future ramifications as their resources changed—for better or for worse—throughout their marriage. For example, one of them might lose his or her job, their home's equity might diminish if the real estate market took a hit, or both.

In your case, living your one best financial life requires two things.

First, you need to have a clear understanding of what you care about most at any given moment.

Second, you must understand what you'd be willing to adjust if you had more or less money to accomplish your goals. In other words, what would you be willing to give up in order to accomplish something that is more important to you?

Understanding what matters to you about money right now, what you want it to do for you, and how you'll achieve as much as possible with your finite resources is an ongoing discussion and a voyage of discovery. And having a systematic way of making good decisions is crucial to realizing positive outcomes throughout your life. After all, you'll continue to make decisions until the day you die. Thus you should expect to make many course corrections over your lifetime.

QUESTIONS TO ASK YOURSELF

- Do you have a defined set of priorities that you want to accomplish in your financial life?
- Do you clearly adjust these goals as your resources change?
- Have you assessed your resources and identified which of your goals can be reasonably accomplished now?
- Do you have a specific way to prioritize and discuss changes in the future with those you love?

JACK REFLECTED ON WHAT HE HAD LEARNED

Up to this point, Jack had never clearly articulated what he wanted to accomplish in his entire financial life, and he hadn't prioritized his financial objectives. As a result, when money came in, he didn't know what adjustments he needed to make. While he often reviewed his income and expense spreadsheets, he neglected to identify how his resources should determine his ability to do—or not do—certain things in life. He immediately related this lesson to his misgivings about his trip to Machu Picchu.

Furthermore, although he recognized that money was a major source of conflict between Olivia and him, he hadn't been able to pinpoint exactly why. After reading the lesson, however, he realized that he and his wife had never discussed the reasons they were working, what they sought to accomplish, and the tradeoffs they'd need to make. For the first time, he understood that having a firm grasp on and control over his priorities was one of the keys to financial peace of mind—an insight that might have prevented the separation.

He clicked the "next" button at the bottom of the page. On the screen that followed, the Alchemist left him space to input a summary of the lesson. Jack quickly scrolled through the pages he had just read, reviewed the illustration, and typed his response.

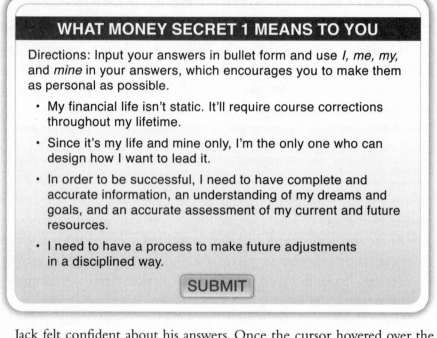

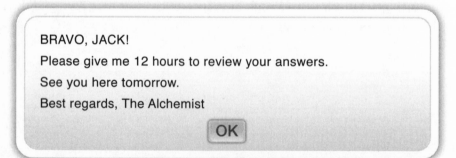

Jack felt confident about his answers. Once the cursor hovered over the "submit" button, however, he experienced trepidation. "What if I answered all these wrong? Will the Alchemist give up on helping me?" he thought to himself. Despite second-guessing, he submitted his responses.

It was an automatic reply, but the confirmation provided relief nonetheless. Jack logged off the site, leaned back in his chair, and wondered what the Alchemist would have to say about his answers.

CHAPTER 6
Jack's Third Lesson

"You are now free to use your electronic devices, and as a courtesy to passengers, we're pleased to offer in-flight WiFi," the flight attendant announced. It would be a quick one-day trip from San Francisco to Los Angeles to meet his client. Jack reached underneath the seat in front of him and grabbed his iPad. He eagerly logged onto the Alchemist's website and couldn't wait to read his comments.

HELLO, JACK!

Great job with your summary points. Enjoy your next lesson.

Remember, take whatever time you need to allow the message to sink in.

Best regards, The Alchemist

< >

He read the short message again, hoping to find a comment from the Alchemist that described how unique—or at least insightful—Jack's summary was. After all, he felt proud of the bullet points he had provided. "I guess no news is good news," he thought to himself. He clicked the "next" arrow, and the following appeared on his screen:

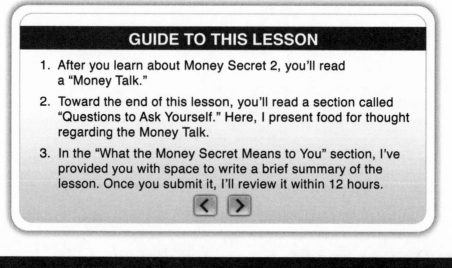

GUIDE TO THIS LESSON

1. After you learn about Money Secret 2, you'll read a "Money Talk."

2. Toward the end of this lesson, you'll read a section called "Questions to Ask Yourself." Here, I present food for thought regarding the Money Talk.

3. In the "What the Money Secret Means to You" section, I've provided you with space to write a brief summary of the lesson. Once you submit it, I'll review it within 12 hours.

< >

MONEY SECRET 2: YOUR ENTIRE LIFE IS DETERMINED BY HOW YOU MAKE DECISIONS.

BIG DECISIONS CAN BE BOTH SCARY AND EXHILARATING

Major decisions can keep you up at night. They sometimes nervously walk the line between big payouts and failures of mythic magnitude. Consider some of the most significant ones you've made in your life. I'll list a few possibilities:

- Who will be my prom date?
- How will I tell my parents about the car wreck?
- What college will I attend?
- Should I take the job?
- Should I quit and start a new career?
- Should I launch my own business?
- Will I get married?
- Will I have kids?
- Do I want a divorce?
- What's the best cancer treatment?
- How will I live the rest of my life?
- What do I do now?

These supersized decisions are stressful because we don't have control over their outcomes. Despite this lack of control, however, we manage to spend an exorbitant amount of time running through countless what-if scenarios. For example, imagine your 21-year-old son calls to share that he has proposed to the woman of his dreams. You do your best to congratulate him, but you struggle with unrestrained approval because you haven't met her. Meanwhile, your gut reaction is to ask, "Honey, what's the rush?" and "Are you sure about this?" but you refrain. Once you end the phone call, you think about your own divorce, and you spend the rest of the night worrying about your son's decision to marry.

I think you'd agree that it's best to make major decisions from a place of objectivity and reason. Unfortunately, when big decisions and uncertainty collide, you've created a mega obstacle called stress. Think of stress as a chemical whose properties are powerful enough to transform objectivity into its opposite—subjective emotion. In other words, when stress dominates your decision making, emotions take the driver's seat. Regrettably, when it comes to the *fear of losing money* or *missing an investment opportunity,* leaning on emotions to drive decisions usually yields negative results.

💲 MONEY TALK: SEEKING SAFETY LEADS TO RUNNING OUT OF RETIREMENT MONEY

"I just don't know what to do!" Julie told her husband. She had just scanned her latest retirement account statement and handed it to him. For the past few months, Julie had watched her savings dwindle. She had spent decades diligently putting away enough in her 401(k) to ensure that she and Keith could have a fantastic retirement.

"I'm just as unsure as you are," her husband said after reviewing the statement. For months, Keith had done his best to ease her anxieties. Despite Keith's best efforts, however, she continued to fear that her shrinking savings would sabotage her plan to retire in three years. And following the seemingly nonstop negative news coverage about the stock market and economy didn't help.

"I can't deal with all this uncertainty. I think I should cut my losses and sell right away," she said.

THINKING THROUGH THEIR CIRCUMSTANCES

For decades, Julie had been carefully investing in her 401(k). The market recently tumbled, and her retirement portfolio lost 30% of its value. With only three years remaining to contribute to her retirement, Julie panicked.

Julie's Big Decision: Can I retire in three years?

Julie's Uncertainty: Will the stock market continue to decline? And how much more will my portfolio's value decrease?

To make matters worse, her husband was in a similar predicament. Constant news reports of Wall Street's weakened state, a global economy in trouble, and friends who were equally despondent only served to heighten Julie and Keith's anxieties. Furthermore, during times of stress, financial or otherwise, Julie's default mode was to seek safety. It stemmed from growing up in a home in which her parents constantly argued about money. Julie now felt that she needed to act fast, and ending her worries became her top priority. Thus she sold all her risky assets and transferred her savings into a money market account. It was a move fueled by her emotions.

Julie's Stress: Fear of losing her nest egg

Julie's Bad Decision: Keeping all of her retirement savings in a money market account

Once she divested from the stock market, a burden lifted off of her. But no sooner had she breathed a sigh of relief than she realized that seeking safety failed to address her big decision: Can I retire in three years? Despite this, Julie stuck by her investment choice and kept the money market account. Over the next few months, the stock market crept up, slowly at first, and then it gained more and more momentum. Within two years, it had fully recovered. By that point, Julie realized that she and her husband would most likely not have enough savings to support themselves. They now had to deal with the consequences of her choice.

UNFAVORABLE OUTCOMES THAT JULIE AND KEITH HAD TO CONSIDER

1. One of us will have to continue to work.
2. We can both retire in three years, but we'll have to significantly cut back our monthly expenses.
3. We won't be able to contribute to our daughter's upcoming wedding.
4. We won't be able to contribute to our grandchildren's college funds.

Sadly, striving for safety caused Julie to run out of money. The result was *less peace of mind*. In addition, she missed the opportunity to grow her retirement savings, and the consequences were irreversible.

❓ QUESTIONS TO ASK YOURSELF

- Do you have a clear way of assessing your emotions when you're making a decision?
- Are you overly concerned about the fear of losing money or the fear of missing opportunities?
- What are the consequences, both immediate and long-term, of the decisions you're making?
- Imagine that you have lost a significant amount of money or that you may miss out on a major moneymaking opportunity. Have you developed a way to make necessary decisions based on sound reasoning rather than fear?
- Do you have mechanisms in place to help you stop yourself from making decisions based on fear?
- Have you and your partner agreed on a way to make good decisions despite stressful circumstances?

JACK REFLECTED ON WHAT HE HAD LEARNED

The Alchemist's lesson reassured Jack that he wasn't alone when it came to making financial mistakes. As much as it was difficult to acknowledge, unless he learned from his past errors, he was prone to make the same ones over and over.

Jack realized that his emotions were powerful triggers that had overwhelmed his judgment during important moments throughout his life. Although he wasn't certain how he'd be able to resist the temptation to act on his emotions, he understood their powerful influence. "Maybe I won't be so swiftly blindsided by my feelings next time," he thought to himself. He looked forward to the solutions that the Alchemist would provide. He clicked the "next" button at the bottom of the window and then typed a summary of the lesson.

WHAT MONEY SECRET 2 MEANS TO YOU

Directions: Input your answers in bullet form and use *I, me, my,* and *mine* in your answers, which encourages you to make them as personal as possible.

- Big decisions and their uncertain outcomes have been major sources of stress throughout my life.
- Stress leads to responses rooted in emotions, which can lead to bad decision making.
- The bad financial decisions I've made in the past have had a lasting impact on my entire life.
- I need a disciplined process to make future decisions.
- Making rational decisions can be very hard when I'm being driven by my emotions. But without an objective perspective, I could fail.

Finally, Jack added the following:

Hey, Alchemist,

Sorry to deviate from your directions, but I wanted to run something by you—why was your response to my summary for Money Secret 1 so brief? Just curious.

–Jack

SUBMIT

Once he clicked "submit," the Alchemist's auto-reply window appeared.

Jack logged out of the website wondering how the Alchemist would respond to his note.

BRAVO, JACK!

Please give me 12 hours to review your answers.

See you here tomorrow.

Best regards, The Alchemist

CHAPTER 7

Jack's Fourth Lesson

As the days passed and the lessons progressed, Jack's respect for the Alchemist deepened. With greater admiration came an increased desire to please his guide. He logged on to the website, eager to read the Alchemist's message.

HELLO, JACK!

Welcome back. I can tell that Money Secret 2 really resonated with you.

With regard to the message you left me last time, this journey is yours and yours only. I'm only here to make sure you're on the right track. So there won't be any grades like you had in school.

My role is to help you make better decisions than you ever have before. Based on what I've read so far, the change is already taking place.

Best regards, The Alchemist

< >

Jack understood that his mentor's goal was to pass on his financial wisdom. So he was only reading the summary to make sure that Jack understood the point of the lesson. He clicked the "next" arrow and read the following page:

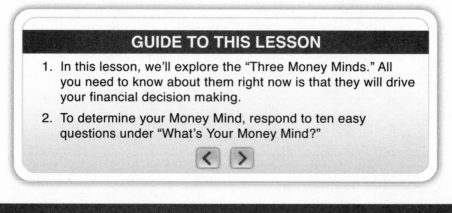

GUIDE TO THIS LESSON

1. In this lesson, we'll explore the "Three Money Minds." All you need to know about them right now is that they will drive your financial decision making.

2. To determine your Money Mind, respond to ten easy questions under "What's Your Money Mind?"

< >

MONEY SECRET 3: YOUR BIASES WILL AFFECT EVERY DECISION YOU MAKE.

💲 MONEY TALK: THE EDUCATION DISCUSSION

"I'll do whatever it takes to make it happen," Michelle told her two friends. Mommy and Me *class had just ended, and the chat among three of the remaining mothers was about their toddlers' education. Kindergarten was still years away, but in their neighborhood, it seemed as if their children's educational paths were set by the time they were born.*

Michelle, Tracy, and Sara all agreed that the local public schools were decent, but from that point their perspectives parted. Michelle continued, "I just can't imagine not giving my girls the best education—no matter what we have to sacrifice."

Tracy disagreed. "I just think it's so much money. I mean, if we spend that on private school every year, what are we going to have left for vacations or to buy a nicer home? Besides, I'm not even sure it's that much better than our public school," she said.

Sara had a different point of view. "Well, I don't think we can afford it anyway—it just wouldn't be financially responsible for us. We wouldn't be able to save anything if we sent our son to private school, and what would happen if I lost my job and couldn't afford tuition? I'd rather save for college and have a rainy day fund," she said.

WHAT'S HAPPENING WITH MICHELLE, TRACY, AND SARA

All three mothers shared the desire to support their children to the best of their ability, they agreed on the benefits of private school, and they came from similar socioeconomic backgrounds. From there, however, their perspectives diverged. Michelle, Tracy, and Sara had different views on what they cared about most, which meant that given the same set of circumstances and information, they'd have completely different ways of making financial decisions.

Michelle's *commitment* to her daughters' education meant that she was willing to make whatever personal sacrifices were necessary in order to provide what she perceived as the best possible schooling for her children.

Tracy's *desire for happiness* meant that although private school appealed to her, she was also concerned about the personal sacrifices she'd have to make. Would she be able to afford a new home, vacations, and costly tuition?

Sara was *fearful* that paying for private school tuition could create additional risk and stress in her life. It might also reduce her financial security, and if she could no longer afford it, her son might have to eventually stop attending.

Could any of them predict whether their final decision would satisfy them? There are certainly no guarantees that any particular approach will ensure a regret-free result. But neglecting to consider multiple perspectives and succumbing to their biases would increase the likelihood of a disappointing, one-sided outcome.

WE EACH HAVE OUR OWN POINT OF VIEW

Everyone perceives his or her financial situation in a particular way. We each have our own perspective that is shaped by our personal history and upbringing. I have already discussed the fact that money helps you do the following three things:

1. **Avoid pain**—by protecting you and helping you to take care of what you're afraid might cause pain in the future
2. **Feel good**—by getting you the things that provide you with happiness and satisfaction
3. **Take care of the ones you love**—by meeting your obligations to family, community, and society at large

We all want money to take care of these things for us. But because of who we are and the life we have led, one of the three is usually more important to us than the other two. And when it comes to important or stressful financial decisions, we generally have a primary focus.

I call this primary focus your **Money Mind**. Think of your Money Mind like a lens you'd find in eyeglasses. You've probably heard the expression about wearing rose-colored glasses. Just as pink glasses would tint everything you saw pink, your dominant Money Mind will do the same for your financial life by influencing your view about every big money decision you'll ever make. Fortunately, while there are endless possible lens colors, there are only three Money Minds. They are as follows:

1. **Fear** (The Protector)
2. **Happiness** (The Pleasure Seeker)
3. **Commitment** (The Giver)

As you may have noticed, the three Money Minds correspond to the trio of things that money will do for us. Each of us has some aspects of all three perspectives, but one usually dominates. Understanding this is key for one simple reason:

When faced with important financial decisions, you will revert to your dominant Money Mind, which will always affect the way you make decisions.

When critical financial matters arise, recognizing the role of your Money Mind is the most important step toward improving your judgment, your behavior, and ultimately the outcome of your decisions. By understanding how your Money Mind biases your thinking, you can prevent poor choices and make more balanced, objective decisions that result in the best possible outcomes. Self-awareness is key to living your one best financial life.

And it helps others, too…

In almost all relationships, the fights you have about money are always the same fight, just about different financial issues. When you understand yourself and how your Money Mind shapes your financial decisions, you can avoid the recurring battles you've had with your loved ones—arguments that arise when each of you relies on your subjective perspective.

For example, one person in a marriage may approach matters from a **Fear Money Mind**, so she'll dwell on what could go wrong in the future. Meanwhile, the other may have a **Happiness Money Mind**, so he'll emphasize what he would like to enjoy today. Or, one person may have a **Commitment Money Mind** and therefore cares deeply about how a financial decision will affect the people he loves, while the other has a **Happiness Money Mind**, so she obsesses about the sacrifices she'll have to make. The table below is a summary of the three Money Minds and what drives each of them:

MONEY MIND	PRIMARY CONCERN	TYPICAL FRUSTRATION
Fear	Protection	Finding peace of mind
Happiness	Satisfaction	Feeling that there's never enough
Commitment	Taking care of others	Too much personal sacrifice

Jack read the chart. He then clicked on the link, MyMoneyCode.com, where the Alchemist provided him with a set of instructions.

Now that I've given you an overview of the three Money Minds, let's take a break from the reading and do a fun exercise. I'm going to ask you ten simple questions that will help you determine your dominant Money Mind.

The questions are multiple choice. Be honest, go with your gut, and don't spend too much time on your answers. Once you're done, click "submit" and you'll get an immediate response.

WHAT'S YOUR MONEY MIND?

QUESTION 1: Well done! You get three great job offers. Which one will you take?

☐ Pays best (A)

☐ Brings you the most joy (B)

☐ Gives you the most time with family (C)

WHAT'S YOUR MONEY MIND?

QUESTION 2: Congratulations! You won $10,000 in game show prize money. You:

☐ Tuck it in your piggy bank (A)

☐ Take a fabulous vacation (B)

☐ Buy a gift for someone you care about (C)

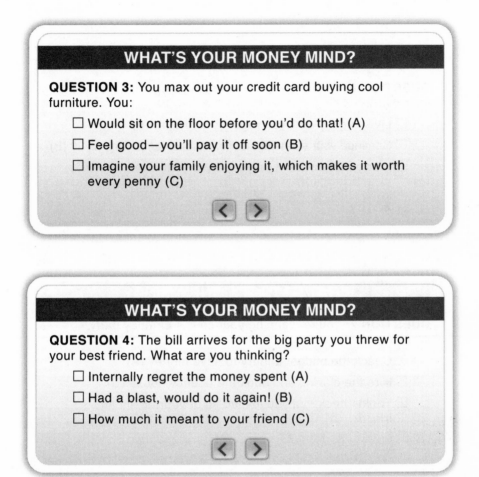

WHAT'S YOUR MONEY MIND?

QUESTION 3: You max out your credit card buying cool furniture. You:

☐ Would sit on the floor before you'd do that! (A)

☐ Feel good—you'll pay it off soon (B)

☐ Imagine your family enjoying it, which makes it worth every penny (C)

WHAT'S YOUR MONEY MIND?

QUESTION 4: The bill arrives for the big party you threw for your best friend. What are you thinking?

☐ Internally regret the money spent (A)

☐ Had a blast, would do it again! (B)

☐ How much it meant to your friend (C)

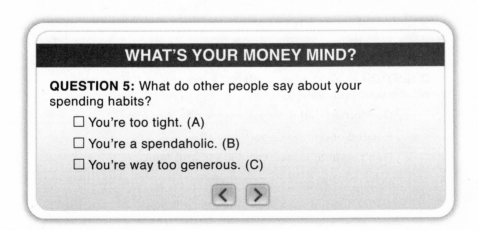

WHAT'S YOUR MONEY MIND?

QUESTION 5: What do other people say about your spending habits?

☐ You're too tight. (A)

☐ You're a spendaholic. (B)

☐ You're way too generous. (C)

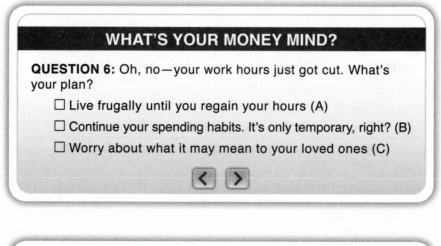

WHAT'S YOUR MONEY MIND?

QUESTION 6: Oh, no—your work hours just got cut. What's your plan?

☐ Live frugally until you regain your hours (A)

☐ Continue your spending habits. It's only temporary, right? (B)

☐ Worry about what it may mean to your loved ones (C)

WHAT'S YOUR MONEY MIND?

QUESTION 7: You're planning your child's birthday party. What's your top priority?

☐ Check the budget and try to save money (A)

☐ Hire the clowns and book the bouncy house (B)

☐ Triple-check that you invited all of your family and friends (C)

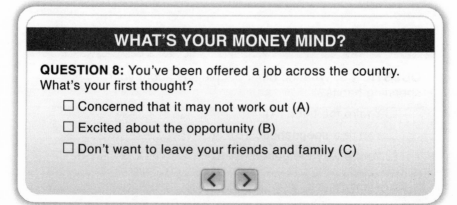

WHAT'S YOUR MONEY MIND?

QUESTION 8: You've been offered a job across the country. What's your first thought?

☐ Concerned that it may not work out (A)

☐ Excited about the opportunity (B)

☐ Don't want to leave your friends and family (C)

WHAT'S YOUR MONEY MIND?

QUESTION 9: Alright! You've just bought your new car. What do you do next?

☐ Wonder if you got the best possible deal (A)

☐ Luxuriate in the new car smell (B)

☐ Can't wait to show it to your friends (C)

< >

WHAT'S YOUR MONEY MIND?

QUESTION 10: Your neighbor has a bigger house and a better car than you. How do you react?

☐ Wouldn't want his or her stress or expenses (A)

☐ Admire his or her success (B)

☐ Why my neighbor? Wish it were mine (C)

SUBMIT

Jack clicked "submit" and couldn't wait to see the results of the questionnaire.

WELCOME TO YOUR MONEY MIND

Jack, here's a breakdown of your answers:

A's — Fear Money Mind: 2
B's — Happiness Money Mind: 6
C's — Commitment Money Mind: 2

Although you have traits of both Fear and Commitment Money Minds, your dominant Money Mind is Happiness, which means that experiencing satisfaction is really important to you.

In the next section, you'll learn about all three. As you read, I encourage you to think about how each Money Mind applies to you and to those you care about most.

After Jack reviewed his results, he returned to the Money Mind questionnaire and answered each item as if he were his wife. He concluded that Olivia was driven by fear. Realizing this gave him a clear understanding of how their different Money Minds generated tension between them—particularly when it came to financial decisions. He continued reading the lesson.

♟ 1. FEAR MONEY MIND: THE PROTECTOR

Amber had just left the car dealership. After test-driving a brand-new white coupe, she knew she had found the car of her dreams. She couldn't wait to call the most important person in her life. "Mom, I know it's a good deal, and the color's perfect, but the monthly payments scare me," she said. Ever since Amber learned to drive, she had always been given hand-me-down cars. Her current VW was ready for the junkyard, and the thought of a brand-new car—her first ever—excited her.

"I think it's time you had a grown-up car, don't you?" her mother asked.

"I think so, too," Amber replied. "That's why I told the salesman that I'd be back tomorrow."

• • •

That night, Amber couldn't sleep. It was 1:00 a.m., and she texted her concerns to her mom: Is this purchase excessive? What if I lose my job? If I continue to save, within a couple of years I can buy the car without having to make payments.

Her mom called her back. "Amber, you've got a great degree, an impressive resume, and plenty in the bank, so even if you did lose your job, I know you'd be fine. Besides, you've been complaining about that beat-up VW for months. I really think everything will be okay." Despite her mom's endorsement of the decision, Amber couldn't help but feel guilty, and her mom knew this. "Don't you think it's time to reward yourself for all your hard work? Honey, stop overanalyzing—Mom's orders," she said.

Once they ended their call, Amber plopped in bed and stared at the ceiling. For the rest of the night, she did her best to ignore the knot in her stomach.

People with a Fear Money Mind are Protectors. A quest for security and peace of mind is what typically drives them. Unfortunately, regardless of the amount of success they attain, *they rarely ever feel secure or satisfied.* This is because no matter how much they have saved, what their income level is, or the opportunities presented to them, they always think in terms of what could go wrong and how to avoid future financial pain.

POSITIVES AND NEGATIVES OF THE FEAR MONEY MIND

The good:

- Typically live well within their means
- Are well prepared for the unexpected
- Are cautious, careful decision makers

Protectors will usually be well prepared for bad situations and are often very responsible stewards of their money. They are careful and deliberate in making decisions and are motivated to protect not only themselves but those whom they care about as well. They also regularly think about various future scenarios that could unfold.

The bad:

- Are slow to make decisions and, as a result, may miss opportunities
- Experience anxiety when facing big commitments
- Make personal sacrifices to maintain security
- Overemphasize delayed gratification and often prepare for bad results that never happen

These individuals will often agonize over big decisions, which can lead to waiting too long to move forward—especially with a major financial decision that carries risk. Even after they act, they will feel anxiety about possible consequences and will wonder whether they made a mistake. And when those around them express doubt, they may stop taking action altogether. In addition, they will make quick shifts to protect themselves—particularly if their plan seems as if it's taking a turn for the worse. In their quest for safety, security, and protection, they may delay gratification, not reward themselves fairly, and overlook themselves and even the people they love.

People with a Fear Money Mind also routinely invest in ideas too late. By the time they feel confident about an investment, it's already made the most gains. They also frequently sell off prematurely. Thus their burning desire to protect can result in them whipsawing in and out of investments.

IF YOU HAVE A FEAR MONEY MIND, YOU CAN IMPROVE YOUR DECISION MAKING BY:

- Understanding that you will almost always envision outcomes that are worse than what actually happens
- Having a method to determine whether or not your fears are rational
- Recognizing that your quest for security can result in excessive personal sacrifice
- Understanding that in order to succeed in anything, some risks need to be taken
- Ensuring that when making financial decisions, your fear is not inhibiting good judgment

It's also important that you don't delay making decisions. While planning for bad outcomes has its benefits, *you must remember that every minute spent protecting is time not spent enjoying.* It's okay to treat yourself well and take pleasure in life, too.

As far as your investments are concerned, you must ensure that your need to protect is not clouding your judgment and causing you to miss opportunities. Whenever the urge to change course arises, you must remind yourself why you invested in something in the first place.

WHEN YOU'RE TALKING TO PROTECTORS:

- Acknowledge and understand how their fears and concerns help to protect everyone from potentially negative outcomes.
- Remind them about the importance of enjoying their lives.
- Reassure them that you are conscious of the potential risks and outline how you will protect each of you from those risks.

When making financial decisions, if you neglect to address the risks and how you will reduce or remove them, people with a Fear Money Mind will most likely feel uncomfortable moving forward. And if they are forced to act against their wishes, they may resent you afterward—especially if things go wrong. In order to communicate effectively, you will need to approach Protectors with a clear description of everything that could go awry and the likelihood of that happening. You also need to address how you will reduce the risks associated with both moving forward and inaction.

2. HAPPINESS MONEY MIND: THE PLEASURE SEEKER

"Can you come with me tomorrow after work?" Sally asked her best friend. The salon owner had just finished walking through the apartment of her dreams and couldn't wait to show it to Mariah. "It's got a killer view, and it's close to everything!" she continued.

"But how much?" Mariah asked.

"Honey, that's why I love you—you're always worried about my spending. If you have to know, it's $2,500 a month," she said.

"I know you're concerned that the salon isn't doing as well as you'd like," Mariah said. "I'd hate for you to commit to something that you wouldn't be able to afford."

Sally appreciated Mariah's perspective. At the same time, she'd been looking for the perfect apartment for months, and who knew when another one like this would be available? Besides, it was closer to her salon, which would cut her commute time in half.

"So can you come with me to see the apartment?" asked Sally.

"Just tell me when," Mariah said. She knew that Sally would most likely sign the lease papers. And as always, Mariah would be there for Sally when she inevitably regretted her decision.

A desire to enjoy what their time and money can provide is what drives those with a Happiness Money Mind. Although their primary quest is to experience satisfaction, they regularly feel that they never have enough money or time. No matter the amount they have saved, their income level, or the opportunities presented to them, they find that there is always something more they'd like to do or enjoy. The thought of having to save for the next big thing frequently leaves them feeling frustrated and impatient.

POSITIVES AND NEGATIVES OF THE HAPPINESS MONEY MIND

The good:
- Are decisive, even with big decisions
- Maximize the pleasure from their resources
- Experience very little anxiety about future problems

Individuals with a Happiness Money Mind will often make big decisions quickly. After making them, they will not spend much time agonizing over the possible consequences. In addition, they tend to emphasize the positives and are quick to see opportunities.

The bad:
- Often feel as though they don't have enough
- Don't spend sufficient time evaluating financial decisions
- Are too casual about future risks
- Overemphasize instant gratification

These Pleasure Seekers are susceptible to making decisions too quickly. They are more prone to worry about missing opportunities than to agonize about losing money. Their decisiveness can lead to creating circumstances in which they live beyond their means or become too comfortable taking on debt.

For example, instead of worrying about high credit card balances, they focus on enjoying life today. They also typically believe that things will work out later. But their perspective may lead them to be overly optimistic despite the contrary opinions of others. This can result in happiness today, but unrestrained, it can also send them down the wrong path later on. In addition, they don't like to delay gratification. Therefore, they regularly speed up the possibility of enjoying things now. They do not spend enough time considering the consequences or the true costs of the decisions they make. As a result, they are often unprepared when negative financial circumstances occur.

IF YOU HAVE A HAPPINESS MONEY MIND, YOU CAN IMPROVE YOUR DECISION MAKING BY:

- Understanding that your perspective may be leading you to be overly optimistic about your circumstances
- Evaluating whether you are thinking objectively about potentially negative outcomes
- Recognizing the importance of conducting objective analysis
- Ensuring that you're not making impulsive decisions based on your need to seek pleasure

If you have a Happiness Money Mind, you should remember to slow down when making financial decisions. While it's wonderful to enjoy the present, you have to be prepared for future challenges as well. It's okay to enjoy yourself and protect yourself, too.

As far as your investments are concerned, you should ensure that your drive to make more money isn't clouding your judgment. Whenever you have the urge to change course, remind yourself why you made the investment in the first place.

WHEN YOU'RE TALKING TO PLEASURE SEEKERS:

- Understand and acknowledge their need to live life to the fullest and enjoy the moment.
- Remind them of the importance of planning and protection.
- Make it clear to them that you're aware of the sacrifices they may need to make, and outline the steps you'll take to ensure that they'll still benefit from the decision over the long term.

It's critical to point out to Pleasure Seekers that their future may include a lot less freedom and choice if they neglect to slow down and consider the true costs and consequences of their decisions. On the other hand, if they're forced to act against their wishes, they may resent you afterward. This is especially true if things turn out differently than expected because it may seem as if their sacrifices were unnecessary. In order to make financial discussions easier, you'll need to approach them with a clear description of the benefits they will realize.

♥ 3. COMMITMENT MONEY MIND: THE GIVER

"Honey, not again! Baby showers, birthdays, weddings—every weekend, it's one thing or another!" Jason said. He wondered when he had forfeited all his free time to family obligations.

His wife, Tricia, had grown used to his complaints. Despite his protest, which was nothing new, she was certain that this time around, he'd be completely okay with the event. "Jay, you know that Travis is my favorite nephew, and we've both talked about how much we love Beth, too," she said. Tricia had promised Travis and his fiancée that she would host an engagement party at their house.

"So if I go along with this, what's the budget?" Jason asked.

"Small enough that we can afford it. But big enough that we may need to tap into our savings," she said. Tricia hoped that he hadn't paid attention to the last part.

"You've got to be kidding. Well, if that's the case, you realize that we may not be able to afford our annual trip," he said.

The news surprised her. "I hadn't really thought about it that way," she said.

People with a Commitment Money Mind are driven by a desire to take care of the people or causes they love. Their primary quest is to find ways they can serve others and help. No matter the amount they have saved, their income level, or the opportunities presented to them, they find that there is always more they can give to those they care about most.

POSITIVES AND NEGATIVES OF THE COMMITMENT MONEY MIND

The good:

- Are generous to those they care about
- Are attentive to other people's needs
- Consider the point of view of others when making decisions

Commitment-focused people are loyal family members, partners, and friends. They are dedicated to meeting the needs of those they love and generously give their time and resources. They consider others' perspectives, not only when it comes to fulfilling obligations but also in terms of how others will be affected by decisions they might make.

The bad:

- Have concerns about "not having enough" time or money
- Neglect to consider personal consequences when making decisions
- Have a desire to always give more
- Overemphasize the opinions of others

Those with a Commitment Money Mind frequently find themselves not having enough time or money to take care of others, regardless of the success they've attained. They routinely sacrifice their own needs in order to fulfill their commitments to others and rely too much on others' perspectives when making decisions. They can be too easily convinced by those with strong opinions and will not think enough about their own needs when making decisions.

Sometimes they're overly casual about important decisions. For example, they'll abdicate significant financial decisions to others rather than play an active role in their own financial lives.

IF YOU HAVE A COMMITMENT MONEY MIND, YOU CAN IMPROVE YOUR DECISION MAKING BY:

- Understanding that people should take responsibility for their own circumstances

- Having a way to honestly assess your needs and then be able to clearly articulate them
- Recognizing the personal sacrifices you make when you give so much to others
- Ensuring that when you're making financial decisions, your desire to please others is not interfering with good judgment

It's also important that you actively participate in decision making. While it's wonderful to be considerate of others, sometimes other people have agendas that are not in line with yours. It's okay to treat yourself well *and* to enjoy life, too.

As far as your investments are concerned, make sure that you consider the view of more than one person. In other words, be certain that you are making a well-balanced decision based on multiple perspectives—including your own.

WHEN YOU'RE TALKING TO GIVERS:

- Empathize with their desire to please and recognize its importance and value.
- Remind them about the need to take care of themselves.
- Ensure that they have honestly expressed their own opinions and thoughts.

When it comes to financial decisions, those with a Commitment Money Mind are typically easy to talk to because they will often understand your perspective. Unfortunately, they sometimes neglect to express their own opinions and meet their own needs. Therefore, you should encourage them to share their views. It's also important that you appreciate and acknowledge their desire to help and fulfill their commitments to others. Lastly, Givers can often be quick to agree with a big decision as long as they feel that those they love have been taken care of. Unfortunately, this approach doesn't always serve a Giver's best interests.

QUESTIONS TO ASK YOURSELF

- Do you know your dominant Money Mind?
- Can you identify situations in the past in which your Money Mind drove financial decisions?
- How would you change those decisions, knowing what you know today?
- Think about the people you care about. Can you identify their dominant Money Minds?

JACK REFLECTED ON WHAT HE HAD LEARNED

Jack realized that all three Money Minds had both good and bad characteristics, and they all profoundly influenced decision making. Everyone, including him, had traits of all three, but one routinely dominated the others. Furthermore, depending on a person's financial circumstances during a particular time, his or her Money Mind could change.

Jack recognized that the biggest challenge with an unchecked Money Mind was that *it would stop him from making balanced decisions.* In order to improve, he would first have to understand the role his dominant Money Mind was playing in a given situation. Then he would need to assess the impact of this natural bias.

Jack understood that his perspective might not change, but he was more aware than ever of how his point of view influenced his decision making. When important financial situations needed to be addressed, rather than allow one Money Mind to drive his financial life, he would be able to consider everything he wanted his money to do for him.

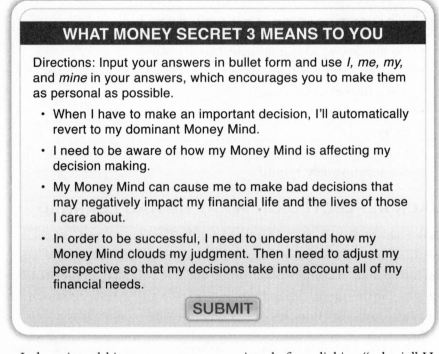

WHAT MONEY SECRET 3 MEANS TO YOU

Directions: Input your answers in bullet form and use *I, me, my,* and *mine* in your answers, which encourages you to make them as personal as possible.

- When I have to make an important decision, I'll automatically revert to my dominant Money Mind.
- I need to be aware of how my Money Mind is affecting my decision making.
- My Money Mind can cause me to make bad decisions that may negatively impact my financial life and the lives of those I care about.
- In order to be successful, I need to understand how my Money Mind clouds my judgment. Then I need to adjust my perspective so that my decisions take into account all of my financial needs.

SUBMIT

Jack reviewed his answers one more time before clicking "submit." He thought about Olivia and their marital separation. He now recognized that his conflicts with his wife about money almost always stemmed from his desire to enjoy (Happiness Money Mind) and her efforts to protect (Fear Money Mind).

Unfortunately, they had never learned to bridge the gap between their different perspectives, which led to both of them feeling alienated and alone. "It's as if we had completely different value systems," Jack thought to himself. He realized that if they had recognized each other's biases, they could have made more balanced decisions with far less conflict.

CHAPTER 8
Jack's Fifth Lesson

The Alchemist's lessons were carrying over into Jack's everyday life. At the supermarket, for example, he thought about his Happiness Money Mind and how it influenced his tendency to buy the expensive bottle of wine versus a similar one on sale. When he hopped online, he noticed how nearly all financial news stories could be distilled to two themes: fears of missing opportunities and fears of losing money. The patterns of his own behavior and what he witnessed in the outside world became predictable—almost amusingly so.

At the same time, his newfound awareness of his own perspective and that of friends, family, and the media was uncomfortable—even downright inconvenient. "Why am I all of a sudden thinking about things that never consumed even a second of my attention before?" he wondered. Perhaps the ignorance of life before the Money Secrets was bliss.

It was that time of day again. Jack logged onto the Alchemist's website. The exercise was becoming routine, but it was far from ordinary.

HELLO, JACK!
Nice summary points. Here's your next lesson.
Can you believe that you're nearly done?
Best regards, The Alchemist

[<] [>]

MONEY SECRET 4: YOU WILL BE DISTRACTED BY THINGS THAT REALLY DON'T MATTER.

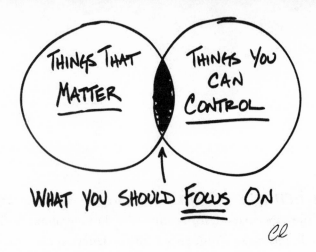

YOUR TWO WORLDS: EXTERNAL AND INTERNAL

With so much competing for your attention every day, determining where to direct your resources is a daunting task. No doubt, there are *limitless* ways to spend your time and energy. Unfortunately, you have a *limited* amount of both. In this regard, time is fair: Whether you're the president of the United States or a newborn infant, your daily dose of 24 hours is the same. Therefore, to reach your goals, you must determine where you'll direct your focus right now and what you'll postpone until later. In this lesson, I'll first describe what is competing for your time and resources when it comes to your financial life. From there, you can determine how to separate essential tasks from nonessential ones.

Each of us lives in two financial worlds: **external** and **internal**. Our **external world** includes taxes, inflation, the country's economy, the stock market, and more. All of these will affect us, but we cannot control them. Meanwhile, our **internal world** consists of our job, salary, spouse, and family—in other words, things we can directly impact.

Both external and internal circumstances are competing for your time every day. When it comes to your external world, you must recognize that you have very limited control over it. For instance, if the government raises taxes or inflation creeps up, there's really nothing you can do about it. Yes, you have the power to vote, but voting can only do so much.

On the other hand, you have the ability to change many aspects of your internal world. If you're dissatisfied with your job, for instance, you can look for something new. Or if you aspire to marry, you can search for your future spouse. Even in your internal world, however, certain things are out of your control. A wife or husband could be diagnosed with cancer, or your children could announce that they're dropping out of college to join the circus. For circumstances that you can't alter, *you can only change how you react to new information.*

CONTROL THE CONTROLLABLE

Imagine that you've planned to lose one pound per week over the next ten weeks. You've made it to week three, and you've proudly stuck to your plan. As a result, you're three pounds lighter. Two activities have caused your weight loss: You've walked three miles a day, and you've cut your total caloric intake.

It's now Monday of week four. At the start of your daily walk, you trip and sprain your ankle. The doctor says that you cannot bear weight on it for two weeks. Suddenly, an accident, which was out of your control, has presented you with two realities:

1. You can't change what happened.
2. You can only change how you react to new information.

For the next 14 days, you can choose to console yourself with donuts and daytime TV, and then scratch your head wondering why you didn't lose any more weight. Or you can come to the conclusion that you have a new set of options before you. Perhaps you'll decide to eat even less because you're unable to walk every day. Or maybe you'll increase your upper-body exercise through resistance training.

Unfortunately, when faced with financial troubles, too many of us agonize over what we *can't* control. We spend our limited time and energy dwelling on a stock market downturn or possible layoffs. Our disbelief or frustration leads to inaction (and perhaps excessive donut consumption). In our idle state, we fail to act on what we can control. Now a bad situation becomes even worse.

THE FOUR THINGS IN YOUR FINANCIAL LIFE THAT YOU CAN CONTROL

The following are key factors that affect your financial life:

1. **Spending**—how much you will live on every day and how much you'll spend to enjoy your life today and in the future
2. **Saving**—how much money you'll put away for the future (often called a safety net or a nest egg)
3. **Timing**—when you'll make major financial changes, such as retiring or paying for major purchases
4. **Taking risk**—how much risk you'll assume with both your money and your assets

All four are inextricably linked. And they're the only things you can really control. For instance, if inflation spikes (external circumstance), you'll have less money to buy the things you want (internal control). It also means you'll probably need to spend less, save more, let your safety net shrink, work longer, take more risk, or some combination of these.

$ MONEY TALK: TOO MANY INVESTMENT OPTIONS, NOT ENOUGH SECURITY

"Buy or rent? And that's just the beginning. There are so many things to think about. Where do we even start?" asked Jennifer. She and her husband had just sold their home and didn't know what to do with the profits that were currently sitting in a non-interest-bearing checking account.

"I'm just not comfortable buying anything right now, especially considering how unpredictable the real estate market is," said Jeff.

"And you know that I'm just as afraid of Wall Street as you are of home ownership," said Jennifer.

Meanwhile, their inaction left them frustrated because they believed that they were missing opportunities. They also knew that a significant part of their savings would support their retirement, which increased the pressure to make a wise decision.

THINKING THROUGH THEIR CIRCUMSTANCES

The couple had earned a hefty profit from the sale of their home. But the volatility of both the stock and real estate markets left them uncertain as to how they'd invest their money. Meanwhile, their savings were sitting in a 0% interest checking account.

Things That Mattered to the Couple: Jennifer and Jeff wanted to live somewhere that was comparable to the home they had recently sold. And as former homeowners, owning their home was a major priority. But given the uncertainty of the real estate market, they were reluctant to buy.

Things They Could Control: The couple knew they had no influence on mortgage interest rates, the fluctuating value of homes, or the ups and downs of Wall Street. This freed them to identify where to direct their attention. They determined that they *could* control things such as how they spent their money and how much to allocate toward retirement. In addition, as Jennifer and Jeff continued to consider whether or not to buy a home, they could increase their safety net and save a portion of their savings for the future.

What They Should Focus On: In order to make a focused and informed decision, Jennifer and Jeff needed a unified way to determine what was important to them. Using the four things in their life that they could control as a guide, they came up with these options:

1. **Spending**—They could use up all of the profits from their home.
2. **Saving**—They could direct all of their money toward retirement savings and their safety net.

3. **Timing**—They could buy another home right away.

4. **Taking risk**—They could invest in the stock market and assume all the risks associated with their investments.

? QUESTIONS TO ASK YOURSELF

- Do you know what matters most to you in your financial life?
- Do you have a clearly defined process to make financial tradeoffs?

JACK REFLECTED ON WHAT HE HAD LEARNED

From the moment he woke up until the time he went to bed, Jack understood that multiple people and circumstances were competing for his attention. Every day, he was pulled in what seemed like a million directions, which often left him wasting time thinking about things over which he had no control.

Jack now realized that when it came to making financial decisions, he could really only control his **spending**, his **savings**, and the **timing** and **level of risk** he would assume. Once he understood that the things he could control could be distilled to a simple four-point list, he experienced a clarity that provided immediate relief. But he wondered about the role that this realization would play in helping him make better decisions. What he was missing was a decision-making process. He then moved on to the last part of the lesson.

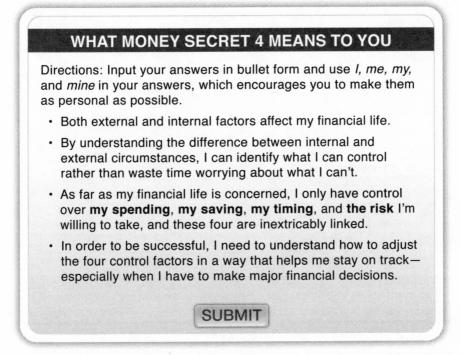

WHAT MONEY SECRET 4 MEANS TO YOU

Directions: Input your answers in bullet form and use *I, me, my,* and *mine* in your answers, which encourages you to make them as personal as possible.

- Both external and internal factors affect my financial life.

- By understanding the difference between internal and external circumstances, I can identify what I can control rather than waste time worrying about what I can't.

- As far as my financial life is concerned, I only have control over **my spending**, **my saving**, **my timing**, and **the risk** I'm willing to take, and these four are inextricably linked.

- In order to be successful, I need to understand how to adjust the four control factors in a way that helps me stay on track—especially when I have to make major financial decisions.

SUBMIT

"Four down and one to go," Jack said as he clicked "submit." He looked forward to what awaited him in the Alchemist's final lesson.

CHAPTER 9
Jack's Sixth Lesson

It was like the last day of a memorable vacation.
On one hand, Jack looked forward to what was ahead. On the other, he was sad to see his daily online exchange with the Alchemist come to an end. He logged on to his computer and wondered how his guide would wrap up this part of their journey.

HELLO, JACK!

You've arrived at your last lesson. I hope that our time together has been fulfilling so far and that you've gained valuable insight into yourself and those you care about.

Best regards, The Alchemist

MONEY SECRET 5: YOU MUST HAVE A GOOD PROCESS TO MAKE GOOD DECISIONS.

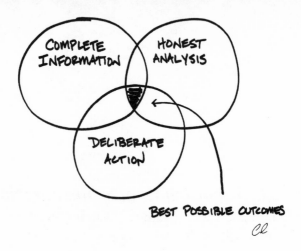

MAKING GOOD DECISIONS

Imagine that you were diagnosed with a life-threatening disease. After the initial shock of the news subsided, you'd be ready to take action. At this point, you'd ask yourself questions such as, "What are my treatment options?" "Are there alternative ways to deal with this illness?" and "What should I include in my overall plan?"

With the first four Money Secrets, you've learned the reasons and motivations behind most of your financial decisions. If this were a medical book, Money Secrets 1 through 4 would have given you the tools to determine what ails you. Now that you've identified the problem—financially speaking—you're ready for the next step. With a clear understanding of the challenges you face, you're prepared to make better, more informed decisions.

THE THREE PARTS TO CREATING THE BEST POSSIBLE OUTCOMES

Whether it's a major decision about your health, your estate, or your finances, in order to realize the best outcome, you need the following:

1. Complete Information
2. Objective Analysis
3. Deliberate Action

1. Complete Information

This means you have a comprehensive understanding of all the issues related to a particular decision you need to make. Complete information includes a decision's possible ramifications, consequences, and long-term costs. You also need an accurate assessment of the resources you have available to pay for your decision.

2. Objective Analysis

In order to move forward in a way that will help you avoid hazardous obstacles, you must remove all personal biases that could cloud your judgment. This is why I had you complete the Money Mind exercise. Now you must have a methodology to assess the costs, benefits, and tradeoffs required to move ahead with your decision objectively.

3. Deliberate Action

Simply put, this will answer the question, "As far as going forward with my proposed decision is concerned, is it yes or no, or both yes and no?" Once you've come to a conclusion, you must follow a clearly defined and well-organized series of action steps in order to realize the best possible outcome. The most systematic way to do this is to have a disciplined process that walks you through all the important steps you need to take.

DIAGNOSE FIRST, PROVIDE SOLUTIONS NEXT

If creating the best possible outcome requires complete information, objective analysis, and deliberate action, and all three are of similar importance, how do you address them equally? *By completing a checklist.*

"Too simple," you might say. A checklist may even seem downright silly. After all, major financial decisions are often head spinning, stomach churning, and insomnia inducing.

WHY ARE CHECKLISTS SO IMPORTANT?

Big decisions often require processing information from diverse and sometimes conflicting sources. Now add the burden of having to act within a particular timeframe, and you've increased the risk of over-looking essential things that will lead to the best possible outcome. By sticking to a checklist, you're ensuring that you're following a consistent system every time a major decision arises.

In Atul Gawande's *New York Times* best-selling book *The Checklist Manifesto,* the author exhaustively researches professionals across a wide range of industries. He describes how they use checklists to maintain re-liable results despite the innumerable variables that can derail a plan. He interviewed building experts who successfully oversaw the construction of skyscrapers. You can imagine the number of people required to turn massive building plans into towering feats of modern engineering: elec-tricians, plumbers, structural engineers, architects—the list of special-ists is mind-boggling. And yet across the globe, skyscrapers of immense complexity are safely housing their tenants.

Hospitals use checklists to make sure that doctors and their support staff perform procedures properly. You've probably heard horror stories of patients who had the wrong leg amputated or their left lung removed rather than the right one. By ticking off items on a list, the hospital staff make sure they are performing surgeries correctly, and they avoid skip-ping basic steps such as maintaining operating-room hygiene.

In Gawande's book, he points to multiple studies that show how checklists have dramatically improved patient safety in hospitals around the world. Regardless of whether it's a major research institution in the United States or a modest facility in the developing world, following simple checklists has saved lives and improved the quality of care that hospitals provide. Thanks in part to *The Checklist Manifesto,* I am a firm believer in the power of checklists. I have used them for nearly every aspect of my business and can attest to their efficacy.

The checklist we'll use covers all parts of the decision-making process. Thus, **Complete Information, Objective Analysis,** and **Deliberate Action** form the checklist's foundation. Its comprehensiveness and simplicity are what make the checklist so useful. Once you've addressed each item on it, you can be assured that you've met the standards for an improved decision-making process.

A CHECKLIST DISCLAIMER: THE TRUTH WILL SET YOU FREE, BUT GETTING THERE ISN'T ALWAYS EASY

At first glance, the checklist will seem simple enough. But simple doesn't necessarily mean effortless. Upon deeper examination, you'll see that it requires you to examine the underlying motivations and objective evidence behind your big decisions.

Once you begin the process, particularly the first time around, you may put down your pen and say to yourself, "Ignorance is way easier than being honest and objective!" And you'd be right...sort of. Certainly in the past, following the same tired habits and blindly depending on your dominant Money Mind have required little mental energy. But if you looked hard at prior behavior, you could probably identify times when the result of mindlessly following old patterns was really not helping you. If you feel frustrated during the checklist process, remind yourself that the benefits outweigh the pitfalls you've encountered in the past—as well as the possible ones you'd face in the future.

If you saw the 1992 blockbuster film *A Few Good Men*, you'll recall that Jack Nicholson's character is on the witness stand at the film's climax. Tom Cruise assaults Nicholson with a series of grueling questions to which Nicholson responds, "You want answers?" and follows with his famous line, "You can't handle the truth!" Don't worry, I won't be yelling at you when we meet, but I agree with his character's point completely. Most of us struggle when it comes to seeing the truth and changing for the better. No doubt the first time you use the checklist will be the hardest. That's why we'll go through it together when we meet. The good news is that with continued use, the process gets easier and easier.

Your commitment to change is one of the main reasons I believed that my lessons would help you. So think of the checklist as the key to the world's finest car. Now imagine tossing the key in the trash and taking a seat behind the wheel. Similarly, unless it's a part of every major financial decision you make, your checklist will be useless.

$ MONEY TALK: THE THERAPY SESSION

"My jaw dropped when I saw the credit card bill," Robert said. He stared at the statement that he brought with him to today's session.

Laura looked across the couch at Dr. Tanner. "See what I'm talking about? It doesn't matter how much I try, he'll always find something wrong," she said.

"I can tell both of you are upset…but for different reasons," Dr. Tanner said. "What frustrated you about the credit card bill, Robert?"

"She spends so much on going out with friends, it's unbelievable!" Robert replied. "I just feel that when it comes to money, she lacks discipline."

"Discipline?" Laura exclaimed. "I work and pay the bills, too, you know. It's not my fault that regardless of how much we save, you think we never have enough. That's not my idea of happiness."

Today's session ran the risk of turning into a back-and-forth blame game. To avoid this, Dr. Tanner directed their attention to the positive: They had solid communication skills in every aspect of their relationship—except when it came to money.

THINKING THROUGH THEIR CIRCUMSTANCES

Robert and Laura needed to have **Complete Information**. Part of this step involved identifying that Robert had a *Fear Money Mind* and Laura had a *Happiness Money Mind*.

Next, an **Objective Analysis** would show that Robert was neglecting to enjoy life and Laura was spending too much money.

Finally, **Deliberate Action** would require them to follow a concrete methodology, one that would ensure that both of their voices were acknowledged and also reflect the tradeoffs each of them would have to make.

JACK REFLECTED ON WHAT HE HAD LEARNED

In order to experience the **Best Possible Outcome,** Jack realized that he needed **Complete Information, Objective Analysis,** and **Deliberate Action.** Fulfilling these three fundamentals required a disciplined and focused methodology. A checklist was the ideal resource, but it would only benefit him if he used it consistently. With a checklist ready to put into action anytime, he would have peace of mind and would improve his entire financial life.

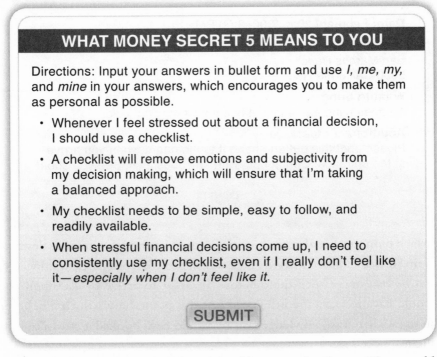

WHAT MONEY SECRET 5 MEANS TO YOU

Directions: Input your answers in bullet form and use *I, me, my,* and *mine* in your answers, which encourages you to make them as personal as possible.

- Whenever I feel stressed out about a financial decision, I should use a checklist.
- A checklist will remove emotions and subjectivity from my decision making, which will ensure that I'm taking a balanced approach.
- My checklist needs to be simple, easy to follow, and readily available.
- When stressful financial decisions come up, I need to consistently use my checklist, even if I really don't feel like it—*especially when I don't feel like it.*

SUBMIT

The five Money Secrets had changed Jack's perspective forever. They would give him the foundation to effectively use the checklist, and the checklist would not only help him to decide about his trip to Machu Picchu but would come to the rescue with future decisions as well. With the five lessons completed, Jack was eager to finally meet the Alchemist. He clicked "submit" and was surprised to receive the following response from his guide:

CONGRATULATIONS, JACK!

You've learned all 5 Money Secrets. Please log in tomorrow morning to see my reply.

Best regards, The Alchemist

The next morning, he read the following:

DETAILS ABOUT OUR MEETING

Date: February 20th, 7:00–8:00 PM

Location:
San Marcos Ranch
5000 California Hwy. 1

What to bring:
An open mind and a jacket because it may get cold

Additional notes:
Please print this out and hand it to the guard when you arrive at the entrance. Contact me with any questions. See you soon!

PRINT

Jack didn't realize that the meeting would be in such a remote destination. He was familiar with the area where San Marcos Ranch was located, but he had never been there before. In order to arrive by 7:00 p.m., he would have to leave the office early. At this point, he was such a believer in the Alchemist's knowledge that he would have booked a cross-country flight if necessary.

CHAPTER 10
Jack Meets the Alchemist

Birthdays were never a big deal for Jack. But this time around, February 20th was a convenient excuse for him to leave the office early. He hopped in his car just in time to avoid rush-hour traffic.

Finally merging onto Highway 1 signaled that he had left the city, its freeways, and urban gridlock behind. To his right was the mighty Pacific Ocean. As he drove, he imagined what San Marcos Ranch looked like. He had heard about the private club before, but its exclusivity made the destination seem far too out of reach to ever bother learning more about it.

His navigation directed him to turn off the main highway and onto a tiny road. When he reached the guard gate, the attendant asked for ID, and Jack handed him the printout from the Alchemist.

"Welcome to San Marcos. To get to the ranch, drive down to the end of the private road. A valet will be waiting for you there," the guard said.

Darkness surrounded Jack as he wound his way along the narrow route. His final destination became brighter and brighter as his car approached the Spanish-style main building, which appeared more five-star resort than rural ranch.

The valet flagged him down. Jack parked next to the young man, who opened his door. "Good evening, sir," he said. "The Alchemist has been waiting for you." Jack stepped out of his car and handed over his keys. The valet pointed him to the club's entrance.

Once in the lobby, a staff member shared that the Alchemist was in the inner courtyard's far right corner under the massive oak tree. "You can't miss it…or him," she said. Jack entered the courtyard, where the warmth from several small fireplaces belied the Northern California winter. The outdoor space was impeccably landscaped and bordered by corridors on all sides.

The Alchemist was browsing his iPad when Jack introduced himself.

"What a pleasure to finally meet. Please, have a seat," the Alchemist said as he pointed to the chair in front of him.

Jack took off his jacket and hung it on the seatback. He imagined a man much older than the person he was finally meeting. The Alchemist couldn't have been more than 50. He was slender and clearly took care of himself.

"How was the drive?" he asked Jack. His warm eyes and welcoming smile suggested that he knew exactly what was on Jack's mind. Jack felt disarmed to be with someone who knew so much about him.

"Beautiful. I enjoyed every moment of it," Jack said. His gaze nervously shifted downward.

A server arrived, and the Alchemist thought that his guest might be hungry. "As you know, we only have an hour together, but don't hesitate to order something to eat," he said.

Anxiety was Jack's most powerful appetite suppressant. "Thanks for offering, but I'll just have water for now," he said. "Speaking of the hour, will I now learn the reason behind it?"

"You mean why so short?" the Alchemist responded. "It's mainly because I wanted to show you that all you needed to know from here on out wouldn't require much of your time."

He added that the several hours Jack had spent on the Money Secrets had provided the strong foundation that made this last step easy to cover.

"So are you ready to begin?" the Alchemist asked.

"Can't wait," Jack said. He sensed his guide's ability to remain undistracted and fully present, which made Jack respect him even more.

The Alchemist put his tablet down, reached into his bag, and handed Jack an iPad. A familiar "Welcome back, Jack!" message glowed on its screen. As always, he input his username and password.

Jack then saw a collection of the "What the Money Secret Means to You" summaries that he had previously provided. As he scrolled through each one, he recalled exactly where he'd been when he had written his responses—at home, in the office, midflight. He smiled as he reflected on everything he had learned in such a short period of time. At the end of the summary, the following appeared:

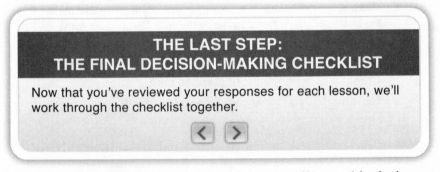

**THE LAST STEP:
THE FINAL DECISION-MAKING CHECKLIST**

Now that you've reviewed your responses for each lesson, we'll work through the checklist together.

Jack took his relationship with the Alchemist offline and looked up at his mentor, whose iPad was on the same screen as Jack's.

"As you recall, Money Secret 5 is, 'You must have a good process to make good decisions.' The checklist we're going to review is your 'good process.' I use checklists not only to help motivated individuals like you but also for nearly every business decision I make," the Alchemist said.

He explained that the main purpose of their meeting was to complete the exercise together. In the end, Jack would know whether or not he should visit Machu Picchu. As they addressed each checklist item, Jack would have an opportunity to ask questions about the process, and the Alchemist would provide his feedback. Jack would then input his answers directly into the app. The following appeared on Jack's screen:

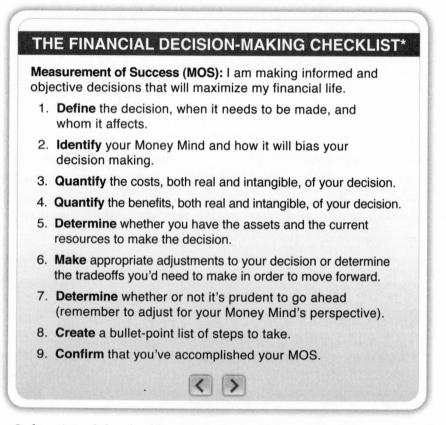

THE FINANCIAL DECISION-MAKING CHECKLIST*

Measurement of Success (MOS): I am making informed and objective decisions that will maximize my financial life.

1. **Define** the decision, when it needs to be made, and whom it affects.
2. **Identify** your Money Mind and how it will bias your decision making.
3. **Quantify** the costs, both real and intangible, of your decision.
4. **Quantify** the benefits, both real and intangible, of your decision.
5. **Determine** whether you have the assets and the current resources to make the decision.
6. **Make** appropriate adjustments to your decision or determine the tradeoffs you'd need to make in order to move forward.
7. **Determine** whether or not it's prudent to go ahead (remember to adjust for your Money Mind's perspective).
8. **Create** a bullet-point list of steps to take.
9. **Confirm** that you've accomplished your MOS.

Jack reviewed the checklist. "I'm surprised it's so short. After reading all the lessons you've provided me, I was expecting something that would be several pages long," he said.

"Keeping it short and sweet took time, but by doing so, it stood the best chance of actually being used," the Alchemist said. "Let's work through this process together, starting with the Measurement of Success."

---

*Follow the directions at the end of this book to create your own custom checklist.

MOS: I AM MAKING INFORMED AND OBJECTIVE DECISIONS THAT WILL MAXIMIZE MY FINANCIAL LIFE.

The Alchemist explained that the goal of the checklist was to ensure that Jack would always make informed and objective decisions that would maximize his entire financial life. Thus the Measurement of Success (MOS) was the first and last step. Regardless of the financial decision, the MOS would remain the same. Once they completed all the items, they would revisit the MOS in order to determine the success of the process. Next, they reviewed the first checklist item together.

> **1. Define the decision, when it needs to be made, and whom it affects.**
> - In one sentence, describe the decision that must be made.
> - Write down the date when it must be made.
> - Write down who will be affected by the decision.
>
>

Jack shared his response to each bullet point: "I really want to visit Machu Picchu, I have to decide a week from Friday, and I think I'm the only one who'll be affected by this decision."

The Alchemist encouraged him to consider who else would be impacted. Jack then added his wife and daughter, his administrative assistant, his clients, and the friends with whom he was traveling. Next, he input the following in his iPad:

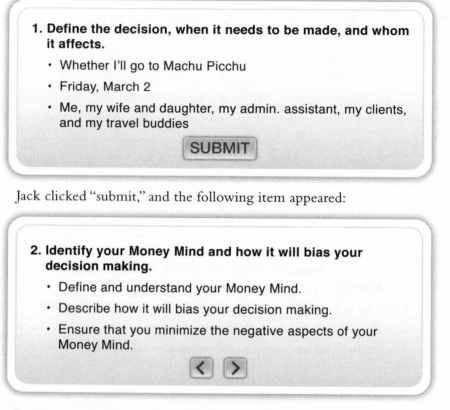

1. **Define the decision, when it needs to be made, and whom it affects.**
   - Whether I'll go to Machu Picchu
   - Friday, March 2
   - Me, my wife and daughter, my admin. assistant, my clients, and my travel buddies

   SUBMIT

Jack clicked "submit," and the following item appeared:

2. **Identify your Money Mind and how it will bias your decision making.**
   - Define and understand your Money Mind.
   - Describe how it will bias your decision making.
   - Ensure that you minimize the negative aspects of your Money Mind.

In Lesson 4, Jack learned that his Money Mind was Happiness. Now the Alchemist asked how this perspective could affect his decision making.

"I'm often so focused on enjoying myself that I can overlook the consequences of my decisions," Jack said. "I also tend to say yes to things that sound fun at first, but I sometimes regret it later on. I really want to be able to make better decisions."

"So in this case, how does your bias influence your decision making?" the Alchemist asked.

"I'm a Pleasure Seeker, so my inclination is to go versus not go," he said.

"Makes sense," said the Alchemist. "Obviously, if you had a Fear Money Mind, your natural inclination would be to *not* go because of the cost. In order to minimize the negative aspect of your Money Mind, you need to slow down and analyze decisions by looking at the pros and cons."

Jack input the following in his iPad:

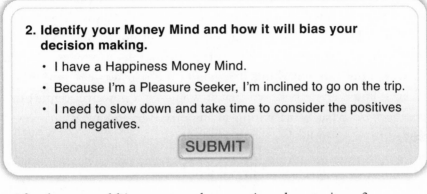

2. Identify your Money Mind and how it will bias your decision making.

- I have a Happiness Money Mind.
- Because I'm a Pleasure Seeker, I'm inclined to go on the trip.
- I need to slow down and take time to consider the positives and negatives.

SUBMIT

After he entered his response, they continued on to item 3:

3. Quantify the costs, both real and intangible, of your decision.

- Outline all the measurable costs.
- Define the intangible costs.
- Remember to consider the costs to all affected parties.

< >

"I think the total cost of the trip will be $6,000, which includes everything from transportation and airfare to meals and hotel—I think I've factored in every expense. But I'm confused about the intangible part," Jack said.

"Since you own a consulting business, would there be any costs associated with your time away?" the Alchemist asked.

Jack's forehead tensed. "Do I really have to answer that?" he asked. His absence from work during his peak revenue-generating weeks could mean that he'd lose clients and not gain new ones.

"I know that the intangibles are tough to determine," said the Alchemist. "But I'm going to ask you to consider even more—and they don't have to be associated with your business."

Jack added that he might end up with credit card balances due to lost income, he might not have enough revenue to follow through with his plan to hire a new consultant, and he might not be able to meet his retirement contribution goals. Another intangible cost would be that his wife, Olivia, might think that taking the trip was irresponsible. In his eyes, however, he believed that it would be a powerful opportunity to reflect on what went wrong in his marriage and what changes he needed to make in his life.

He reluctantly input the following in his iPad:

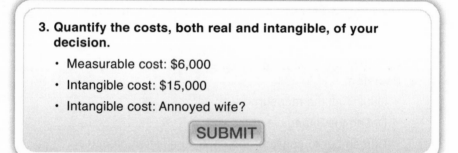

3. Quantify the costs, both real and intangible, of your decision.

- Measurable cost: $6,000
- Intangible cost: $15,000
- Intangible cost: Annoyed wife?

SUBMIT

Jack was relieved that checklist item 3 was behind him. He began to think that the Alchemist was trying to talk him out of taking the trip. He then read the next checklist item:

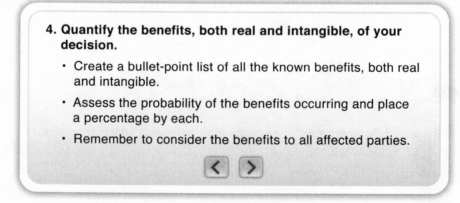

4. Quantify the benefits, both real and intangible, of your decision.

- Create a bullet-point list of all the known benefits, both real and intangible.
- Assess the probability of the benefits occurring and place a percentage by each.
- Remember to consider the benefits to all affected parties.

< >

One benefit he immediately identified was that he looked forward to spending time with his friends and relaxing. He then addressed each of the bullet points in checklist item 4.

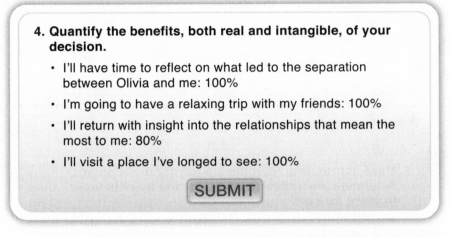

4. Quantify the benefits, both real and intangible, of your decision.
- I'll have time to reflect on what led to the separation between Olivia and me: 100%
- I'm going to have a relaxing trip with my friends: 100%
- I'll return with insight into the relationships that mean the most to me: 80%
- I'll visit a place I've longed to see: 100%

SUBMIT

"And how will all affected parties benefit?" the Alchemist asked.

Jack believed that he and his friends would be incredibly happy to spend time together. "We'll make lifelong memories. And maybe I can even figure out how to save my marriage," he said. They then moved on to checklist item 5.

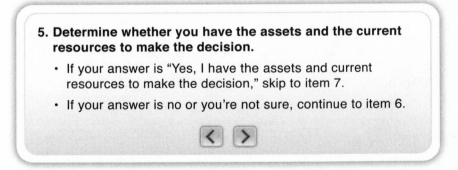

5. Determine whether you have the assets and the current resources to make the decision.
- If your answer is "Yes, I have the assets and current resources to make the decision," skip to item 7.
- If your answer is no or you're not sure, continue to item 6.

"I have savings to cover the $6,000 cost of the trip, but I'll be in trouble when I get back because of the reduced income," Jack said. He was referring to the revenue-generating opportunities that he would miss as a result of being away on vacation. "I can't afford to give up $15,000 in income without maxing out my credit cards and really having to rein in my spending for the rest of the year."

He typed the following in his iPad:

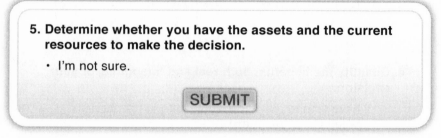

5. Determine whether you have the assets and the current resources to make the decision.

 • I'm not sure.

SUBMIT

"Fortunately, item 6 will address your concerns," the Alchemist said. Jack read the following:

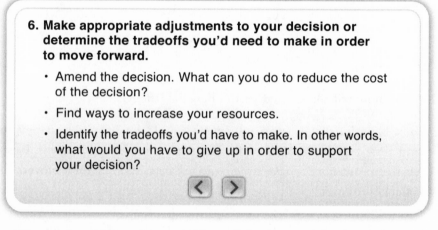

6. Make appropriate adjustments to your decision or determine the tradeoffs you'd need to make in order to move forward.

 • Amend the decision. What can you do to reduce the cost of the decision?

 • Find ways to increase your resources.

 • Identify the tradeoffs you'd have to make. In other words, what would you have to give up in order to support your decision?

"Remember Money Secret 4: *You will be distracted by things that really don't matter.* There are four things in your financial life that you can control:

1. Spending
2. Saving
3. Timing
4. Taking risk

"As far as your trip is concerned, since you don't have any hidden savings, all you can control is your spending and your timing," the Alchemist said. He suggested that Jack could shorten his vacation and commit to working harder when he returned.

"I was planning on taking a trip next New Year's, and I think I should cancel it," Jack said, "Regarding Machu Picchu, instead of going for 14 days, I could go for 10—from Friday to the following Sunday. That way, I'd only miss one real workweek." He realized that shortening his trip would cut his missed work opportunities in half, from $15,000 to $7,500.

In terms of one of his biggest expenses, he knew he ate out too often. If he cooked for himself and his daughter until the trip, he could easily save another $1,000. The brainstorming session provided immediate relief from his anxieties. "I think I can actually make this work," he said. Jack input the following in his iPad:

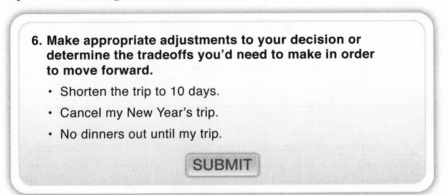

6. Make appropriate adjustments to your decision or determine the tradeoffs you'd need to make in order to move forward.

• Shorten the trip to 10 days.

• Cancel my New Year's trip.

• No dinners out until my trip.

SUBMIT

"You're making the kinds of tradeoffs that will maximize your peace of mind and minimize your anxiety," the Alchemist said.

Overall, Jack was surprised that he'd only have to make three adjustments. He realized that the minor changes would reduce his trip expenses from $6,000 to $5,000. He would also save $7,500 in work costs, and he would be able to generate additional revenue during the holidays to pay for this entire trip. And cutting four days from his vacation would allow him to go without feeling that he was being financially irresponsible.

He leaned back in his seat and took a deep breath. He reflected on past financial decisions and realized how taking such a calm, deliberate approach to decision making would have improved his entire life. Jack and the Alchemist then addressed the next checklist item.

7. Determine whether or not it's prudent to go ahead (remember to adjust for your Money Mind's perspective).

"Definitely!" was Jack's immediate response. And for the first time, it wasn't just his pleasure-seeking Money Mind telling him that. He input Y-E-S as his response to item 7, confident that he had come up with a prudent plan that would result in returning home from his trip with peace of mind rather than regret. He and the Alchemist then addressed the next checklist item:

8. Create a bullet-point list of steps to take.

"Let's go through your next steps together," the Alchemist said. Jack shared his answers and then typed them in his iPad.

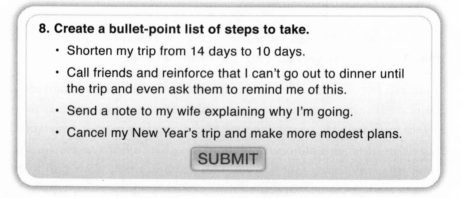

8. Create a bullet-point list of steps to take.

- Shorten my trip from 14 days to 10 days.
- Call friends and reinforce that I can't go out to dinner until the trip and even ask them to remind me of this.
- Send a note to my wife explaining why I'm going.
- Cancel my New Year's trip and make more modest plans.

SUBMIT

He clicked "submit," and the last item appeared.

9. Confirm that you've accomplished your MOS: I am making informed and objective decisions that will maximize my financial life.

SUBMIT

"Do you feel like you've made an informed and objective decision?" the Alchemist asked.

"Absolutely," Jack said.

The Alchemist looked down at his wristwatch. "And this only took us 40 minutes. If you want, we can spend our remaining time together addressing any questions you have," he said.

Q & A WITH THE ALCHEMIST

Jack had several questions and was eager to have the opportunity to ask them. But first he wanted to share an observation.

"To be completely honest, I feel kind of silly. Shouldn't I have been able to come to these conclusions on my own, without the checklist? After all, I'm a grown man, am educated, and deal with much more complicated problems at work every day. At the same time, I realize that as far as my personal financial life is concerned, I've never had a sound decision-making process," he said.

The Alchemist responded, "It's pretty remarkable how we need to be reminded how to do things correctly once in a while, isn't it?"

Next, Jack asked what the most common challenges to using the checklist were.

"Being objective is probably the hardest part," the Alchemist answered.

He explained that Jack would eventually feel as though he could make big decisions without the checklist, once the process became second nature. "But what I've found is that people who are financially successful over the long term know how important it is to stay open-minded and disciplined.

They realize their weaknesses and take the necessary steps to remain objective. Does that answer your question?" he asked.

"It's hard to admit this, but part of me is full of regret right now," Jack said. "Had my wife and I been able to communicate about money, we might not be separated today. How could we have done things differently?"

"I was hoping you'd ask," the Alchemist said. "In your iPad, I've loaded a checklist for couples. Basically, all you need to do is complete the exercise individually...just as we've done today. You then come together, hear each other's perspective, and agree on each of the important steps." He helped Jack find the checklist in his iPad. The following appeared on Jack's screen:

DECISION-MAKING CHECKLIST FOR COUPLES*

Measurement of Success (MOS): We are making informed and objective decisions that we both agree will maximize our financial life.

1. Each person completes the "Financial Decision-Making Checklist."

2. Participants take turns sharing the results of their entire checklist.

3. If necessary, each person asks clarifying questions.

4. Jointly quantify the costs, both real and intangible, of the decision.

5. Jointly quantify the benefits, both real and intangible, of the decision.

6. Determine whether you both have the assets and current resources to pay for the decision. If not, complete item 7.

7. Make appropriate adjustments to your decision or determine the tradeoffs you'd need to make in order to move forward.

8. Come to a mutual agreement regarding the action steps you must take.

9. Confirm that you've accomplished your MOS.

⟨ ⟩

*Follow the directions at the end of this book to create your own custom checklist.

Jack read through the checklist and looked up at the Alchemist. "Yet again, I'm surprised by the checklist's simplicity," he said.

"Simple—yes, but it's not always easy," the Alchemist said. "When you're dealing with two people, you have double the emotions. The biggest challenge is to be aware of how you react to one another." He added that most emotions that come up because of money are usually related to a person's perspective. For couples to effectively complete the checklist, *they both need to speak the language of the other person's Money Mind*. And if the conversation starts to heat up, it's probably time to take a break.

"What do you mean by *speak the language* of the other person's Money Mind?" Jack asked.

"For instance, you have a Happiness Money Mind, which means that you're a Pleasure Seeker," the Alchemist responded. "If we were making a decision together, I'd need to first recognize the importance you place on enjoying life. Once you saw that I understood your perspective, I'd be better able to remind you of the consequences of your Money Mind. I must also ensure that our final decision addresses all of your concerns. Now, let's say that I had a Fear Money Mind. It would be important for you to recognize my need for protection and safety."

In addition, dominant personalities often had difficulty allowing others to have different perspectives. The Alchemist was convinced, however, that if a couple followed through with the process, both people would feel understood and fairly treated—even if one of them was not completely satisfied with the final decision.

"What happens if a couple both have the same Money Mind?" Jack asked, "for instance, if they both have a Fear Money Mind. I bet they never fight about money."

"You may be right. Perhaps they don't argue, but they sure aren't making good decisions, either," the Alchemist said. "When both of them are concentrating on protecting for the future, it's unlikely that they are enjoying life today as much as they could. After all, the entire point of the process is to ensure that everyone is taking a balanced approach."

The Alchemist glanced at his wristwatch. "Looks like we're about out of time," he said.

"I don't know how to thank you," Jack said.

"I've got a simple request: Improve the lives of the people you touch," he responded.

Jack recalled how he had received the Alchemist's business card from his sister. "Does that also mean that it's my turn to give your card away?" he asked.

"One person, one hour," the Alchemist said.

They stood up and shook hands. Jack then made his way to the entrance of San Marcos Ranch. His car was already waiting for him in front. The valet opened his door, and Jack took a seat.

"Have a great evening, and drive safely," the attendant said as he closed the door.

Jack turned to his right and noticed a file folder on the passenger's seat. Inside was a cover letter.

Dear Jack,

It was great to finally meet you.

I've enclosed a copy of the checklists for both individuals and couples. I've also emailed them to you.

I genuinely hope that making good financial decisions will become second nature to you and that the work you've done improves your life. Anytime you have a question, go to MyMoneyCode.com. I've got amazing tools waiting for you there. And I look forward to continuing our connection through the next person who receives my business card.

It's been a pleasure to guide you in your journey to live your one best financial life.

Warmest regards, The Alchemist

Jack grabbed his phone, opened his Twitter app, and typed the following:

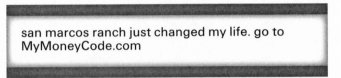

san marcos ranch just changed my life. go to
MyMoneyCode.com

The pithy post was meant more for him—to remind him of what he had just experienced. But no sooner had he input his update than his phone rang. His sister's photo appeared on the screen, and he answered the call.

"I assume you just saw my tweet," Jack said.

"Feel better?" Claudia asked. Her voice echoed through the car's speakers.

"Completely," he said.

"Tell me all about it," she said.

"I can't wait to, but before I dive into it, do you mind if I give Olivia a call first? I think we need to talk," he said.

"I wouldn't want it any other way," Claudia said.

He ended their conversation and sent a voice command to his car: Dial my wife.

Jack listened to his phone ring as he made his way toward the main highway. He felt his heart pound in his chest as he thought about what he should say.

"Jack, is that you?" Olivia asked.

"Yeah, it's me. I'm so happy you picked up. Can we talk?" he asked.

He glanced in the rearview mirror and saw the lights of San Marcos Ranch fade behind him.

CHAPTER 11
Afterword:
A Bit About the Author's Life

For as long as I can remember, I've been driven by raging fear and insecurity. This comes as a surprise to many, even those who have known me for years. After all, my bio's bullet points could come straight out of the playbook of the American Dream: I arrived in the U.S. with modest means, no connections, and a foreign accent; I worked through college; I earned my degrees and went on to build a thriving business; I sold it for a small fortune and started another company that was even more successful than the first one. But after each milestone, rather than mark the moments by celebrating, I'd panic. Thoughts like, "What if I lose it all?" and "Something's bound to go wrong at any moment!" would keep me up at night.

Contrast that mindset with the optimistic outlook of my wife, who is always confident that regardless of what happens, everything will work out in the end. In fact, the gap between our perspectives sometimes seems as wide as the space separating my African homeland from the U.S. For example, in 2001, at 34 years old, I formally left the company I had helped to create and lead. At the time, General Electric Financial had bought us out for millions of dollars. The acquisition by one of the world's largest companies fulfilled a goal that I'd set for myself 20 years ago as a kid living a continent away.

CHILDHOOD IN AFRICA

I was lying in bed listening to my parents' arguing fill the house. This signaled that it was time to clutch my pillow and cover my ears. Tonight's blowup was about my teeth.

"You know he needs braces. But with the way you spend money, there's no way we'll be able to afford them," my mom said.

"Don't get started," my dad said, each word louder than the one before it.

"Maybe if you'd stop spending so much, I wouldn't have to!" she said.

Little did that 10-year-old boy know that he'd have to wait 2 decades for his wonky teeth to straighten out. It wasn't until I was 30 years old and living in the U.S. that I could finally afford to get them fixed, though by then they were practically a badge of merit!

Another night, their yelling match would be about potentially losing the house. Yet another time, they'd quarrel over bills that were piling up. On any given day of the week, even the calmest conversation between them would escalate into a screaming match. Every fight was a variation on a predictable theme: My mom was terrified of not having enough money, and my dad believed that we had plenty of cash to do whatever he wanted.

The arguing ended when I was 11 years old. That year, my dad was hospitalized after a motorcycle accident. Interestingly, the collision gave my mom the strength to do what she'd wanted to do for years—leave my father. They divorced and sold the house. She was nearly broke and had to open a line of credit to pay rent. My mom, two sisters, and I moved into a tiny cottage where we all slept on mattresses laid out on the living room floor. Shortly after the split, my mom shared two important facts with me.

1. Now that your dad's gone, you're the man of the house.
2. Your dad regularly beat me up throughout our marriage.

Point two shed light on the excuses she'd given me before:

"Ran into a closet door," she said, turning her blackened eye to the floor. "Your mom can be so clumsy, can't she?" I now understood that it was one of many cover-ups I'd heard growing up.

During the weekends, my sisters and I stayed with my father. Now that my mom wasn't around to bear the brunt of his abuse, I became his next target. For those next few years, he regularly took his rage out on me. Fortunately, my sisters were spared physical harm. In exchange, they would have to watch him beat up their brother.

My dad's apartment was even smaller than my mom's home. The studio sat above a Chinese restaurant in a low-rent strip mall, and the smell of hot grease permeated the living space. Unfortunately, his lack of savings and the motorcycle accident had wiped him out financially. He was desperate and enlisted us to help pay the bills. On Saturdays, he would walk us to a thrift store with his possessions in hand, such as old electronics, small pieces of furniture, and knickknacks.

"Look sad. Look poor. Do whatever it takes to get the most money," he said. The words were meant to inspire the three of us to do good work—call it a sales manager's pep talk. The dull ache in my gut grew stronger as I got closer and closer to the entrance. My two sisters—five and ten years old at the time—and I braced ourselves as we entered "Snippets." The secondhand store reeked of stale clothing and dust. Once our task was complete, we'd leave Snippets and meet our father, who waited for us outside. We handed him the results of our labor. Within hours, my dad would spend everything we had earned for him. But before he blew it all, he'd treat us to ice cream or a modest meal. It was a reward that only my free-spirited five-year-old sister truly appreciated.

EXTERNAL POLITICAL UNREST

On the inside, the homes where I grew up were often loud, violent places. But that didn't explain why, at age 11, I had my own gun. The world outside our four walls was a terrifying place. Rhodesia was in the midst of a civil war whose bitter conclusion created a new country, the Republic of Zimbabwe. The years of conflict meant that our lives were at risk every day. For instance, in the U.S., the yellow school bus may not always feel safe to kids who are teased by their peers. But such bullying pales in comparison to the place where I'm from. Daily shootings, raids, and killings meant that our school commute required a military convoy. Every morning, my sisters and I would hop in our parents' car and join the other kids who went off to school. Armored military escorts flanked both sides of the caravan.

Early curfews and lights-out marked every evening. A couple of times a week, a third layer was added to our police state—enforced silence. Our voices couldn't grow louder than a whisper. Despite these conditions, my sisters and I still had fun; it's amazing how children can find ways to entertain themselves in any situation. In our silent play, we'd quickly have to cover our mouths to muzzle any spontaneous laughter. Those nights, the moonlit sky, the crickets, and our hushed voices filled the evening void. On occasion, the quiet was interrupted by gunfire, shouting, and fear that surged inside us.

Given the stress I experienced both inside and outside my home, I'm sure that it won't come as a surprise to any of you why fear and insecurity have dominated my outlook. To my wife's chagrin, it took me far too long to figure out how to work with my personal struggles rather than blindly react to them.

"Honey, let's celebrate by taking a nice, long trip with the family," my wife suggested shortly after I'd left the company that was purchased by G.E. Financial. "This would be the perfect chance to spend time with the girls before they get really serious about school."

From my point of view, however, any celebration would be premature. It would be like blowing out the birthday candles before we even bought the cake. Sadly, it took me years to finally recognize that no matter how significant my professional accomplishments were, there would always be something else to worry about, some other impending disaster to prepare for, and yet another reason to remain vigilant. Addressing pressing situations, both real and not yet realized, always took precedence over relishing a major achievement. In my mind, celebrating was something that I could always do later. But time and time again, "later" never came.

Fortunately, I've worked with several mentors and guides over the last few years. As a result, I recognized how my fears and insecurities were paralyzing me and limiting the happiness that I could experience at any moment. And I also realized that simply being aware was enough to change my behavior forever. In fact, I'm convinced that being honest and objective and having discipline can change any person.

Since feeling completely helpless at age 11, I've been blessed beyond words every day of my life. It's my desire to share what little I've learned to help the people I touch, which explains why the profits of this book will go to causes that improve the lives of people around the world.

The Money Code Resources

CHAPTER 1. THE PROBLEM WITH MONEY
MONEY: WHAT'S IT GOOD FOR?

Here's the simple truth about money—it can really only help you
do three things in your life:

1. **Avoid pain**—by protecting you and helping you to take care of what
   you're afraid might cause pain in the future
2. **Feel good**—by getting you the things that provide you with
   happiness and satisfaction
3. **Take care of the ones you love**—by meeting your obligations
   to family, community, and society at large

CHAPTER 3. THE BACKGROUND CHECK
THE FOUR HONEST QUESTIONS
ABOUT YOUR FINANCIAL WELLNESS

1. Do you avoid making decisions about money?
2. Do you feel as though you're missing something in your
   financial life?
3. Have you made money decisions you've regretted and then
   repeated the same mistakes?
4. Does talking about money with the people you love make you feel
   uncomfortable?

THE TWO ETERNAL TRUTHS
ABOUT DECISION MAKING

1. Lack of clarity and understanding of yourself and the situation
   at hand will lead to poor decisions.
2. Creating lasting change requires you to be honest with yourself and
   to be disciplined and persistent.

CHAPTER 4. JACK ENTERS
THE ALCHEMIST'S WEBSITE

Every financial decision is driven by one of two fears:
- **Fear of missing opportunities**
- **Fear of losing money**

CHAPTER 8. JACK'S FIFTH LESSON
THE FOUR THINGS IN YOUR FINANCIAL LIFE
THAT YOU CAN CONTROL

1. **Spending**—how much you will live on every day and how much you'll spend to enjoy your life today and in the future
2. **Saving**—how much money you'll put away for the future (often called a safety net or a nest egg)
3. **Timing**—when you'll make major financial changes, such as retiring or paying for major purchases
4. **Taking risk**—how much risk you'll assume with both your money and your assets

---

THE FIVE MONEY SECRETS

I. YOUR LIFE WILL BE FILLED WITH TOUGH CHOICES.

2. YOUR ENTIRE LIFE IS DETERMINED BY HOW YOU MAKE DECISIONS.

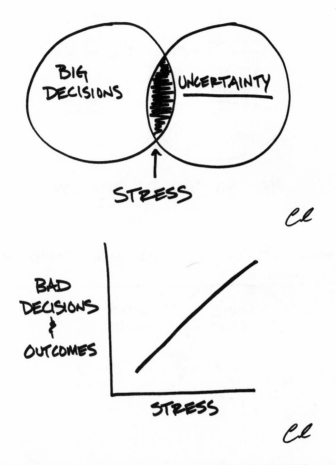

3. YOUR BIASES WILL AFFECT EVERY DECISION YOU MAKE.

MONEY MIND	PRIMARY CONCERN	TYPICAL FRUSTRATION
Fear	Protection	Finding peace of mind
Happiness	Satisfaction	Feeling that there's never enough
Commitment	Taking care of others	Too much personal sacrifice

4. YOU WILL BE DISTRACTED BY THINGS THAT REALLY DON'T MATTER.

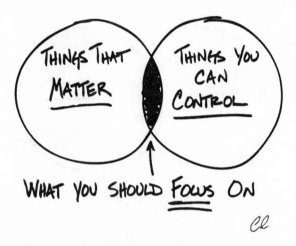

5. YOU MUST HAVE A GOOD PROCESS TO MAKE GOOD DECISIONS.

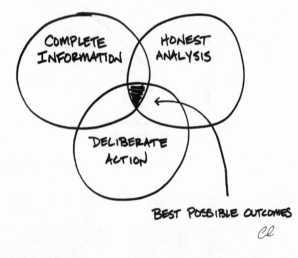

WHAT'S YOUR MONEY MIND?

QUESTION 1: Well done! You get three great job offers. Which one will you take?

☐ Pays best (A)

☐ Brings you the most joy (B)

☐ Gives you the most time with family (C)

QUESTION 2: Congratulations! You won $10,000 in game show prize money. You:

☐ Tuck it in your piggy bank (A)

☐ Take a fabulous vacation (B)

☐ Buy a gift for someone you care about (C)

QUESTION 3: You max out your credit card buying cool furniture. You:

☐ Would sit on the floor before you'd do that! (A)

☐ Feel good—you'll pay it off soon (B)

☐ Imagine your family enjoying it, which makes it worth every penny (C)

QUESTION 4: The bill arrives for the big party you threw for your best friend. What are you thinking?

☐ Internally regret the money spent (A)

☐ Had a blast, would do it again! (B)

☐ How much it meant to your friend (C)

QUESTION 5: What do other people say about your spending habits?

☐ You're too tight. (A)

☐ You're a spendaholic. (B)

☐ You're way too generous. (C)

QUESTION 6: Oh, no—your work hours just got cut. What's your plan?

☐ Live frugally until you regain your hours (A)

☐ Continue your spending habits. It's only temporary, right? (B)

☐ Worry about what it may mean to your loved ones (C)

QUESTION 7: You're planning your child's birthday party. What's your top priority?

☐ Check the budget and try to save money (A)

☐ Hire the clowns and book the bouncy house (B)

☐ Triple-check that you invited all of your family and friends (C)

QUESTION 8: You've been offered a job across the country. What's your first thought?

☐ Concerned that it may not work out (A)

☐ Excited about the opportunity (B)

☐ Don't want to leave your friends and family (C)

QUESTION 9: Alright! You've just bought your new car. What do you do next?

☐ Wonder if you got the best possible deal (A)

☐ Luxuriate in the new car smell (B)

☐ Can't wait to show it to your friends (C)

QUESTION 10: Your neighbor has a bigger house and a better car than you. How do you react?

☐ Wouldn't want his or her stress or expenses (A)

☐ Admire his or her success (B)

☐ Why my neighbor? Wish it were mine (C)

DIRECTIONS

Once you mark your answers, tally your A's, B's, and C's.

A's (Fear): _____

B's (Happiness): _____

C's (Commitment): _____

My dominant Money Mind is: _____

For more information, see Chapter 7: Jack's Fourth Lesson, and to learn more about your Money Mind, go to MyMoneyCode.com.

THE FINANCIAL DECISION-MAKING CHECKLIST FOR INDIVIDUALS (OVERVIEW)*

Measurement of Success (MOS): I am making informed and objective decisions that will maximize my financial life.

1. **Define** the decision, when it needs to be made, and whom it affects.
2. **Identify** your Money Mind and how it will bias your decision making.
3. **Quantify** the costs, both real and intangible, of your decision.
4. **Quantify** the benefits, both real and intangible, of your decision.
5. **Determine** whether you have the assets and the current resources to make the decision.
6. **Make** appropriate adjustments to your decision or determine the tradeoffs you'd need to make in order to move forward.
7. **Determine** whether or not it's prudent to go ahead (remember to adjust for your Money Mind's perspective).
8. **Create** a bullet-point list of steps to take.
9. **Confirm** that you've accomplished your MOS.

THE FINANCIAL DECISION-MAKING CHECKLIST FOR INDIVIDUALS (EXTENDED VERSION)

Measurement of Success (MOS): I am making informed and objective decisions that will maximize my financial life.

1. **Define** the decision, when it needs to be made, and whom it affects.
   - In one sentence, describe the decision that must be made.
   - Write down the date when it must be made.
   - Write down who will be affected by the decision.
2. **Identify** your Money Mind and how it will bias your decision making.
   - Define and understand your Money Mind.
   - Describe how it will bias your decision making.
   - Ensure that you minimize the negative aspects of your Money Mind.

Follow the directions at the end of this book to access your own checklist.

THE FINANCIAL DECISION-MAKING CHECKLIST FOR INDIVIDUALS (EXTENDED VERSION) CONTINUED

3. **Quantify** the costs, both real and intangible, of your decision.
   - Outline all the measurable costs.
   - Define the intangible costs.
   - Remember to consider the costs to all affected parties.

4. **Quantify** the benefits, both real and intangible, of your decision.
   - Create a bullet-point list of all the known benefits, both real and intangible.
   - Assess the probability of the benefits occurring and place a percentage by each.
   - Remember to consider the benefits to all affected parties.

5. **Determine** whether you have the assets and the current resources to make the decision.
   - If your answer is "Yes, I have the assets and current resources to make the decision," skip to item 7.
   - If your answer is no or you're not sure, continue to item 6.

6. **Make** appropriate adjustments to your decision or determine the tradeoffs you'd need to make in order to move forward.
   - Amend the decision. What can you do to reduce the cost of the decision?
   - Find ways to increase your resources.
   - Identify the tradeoffs you'd have to make. In other words, what would you have to give up in order to support your decision?

7. **Determine** whether or not it's prudent to go ahead (remember to adjust for your Money Mind's perspective).

8. **Create** a bullet-point list of steps to take.

9. **Confirm** that you've accomplished your MOS.

DECISION-MAKING CHECKLIST
FOR COUPLES

Measurement of Success (MOS): We are making informed and objective decisions that we both agree will maximize our financial life.

1. Each person completes the "Financial Decision-Making Checklist."
2. Participants take turns sharing the results of their entire checklist.
3. If necessary, each person asks clarifying questions.
4. Jointly quantify the costs, both real and intangible, of the decision.
5. Jointly quantify the benefits, both real and intangible, of the decision.
6. Determine whether you both have the assets and current resources to pay for the decision. If not, complete item 7.
7. Make appropriate adjustments to your decision or determine the tradeoffs you'd need to make in order to move forward.
8. Come to a mutual agreement regarding the action steps you must take.
9. Confirm that you've accomplished your MOS.

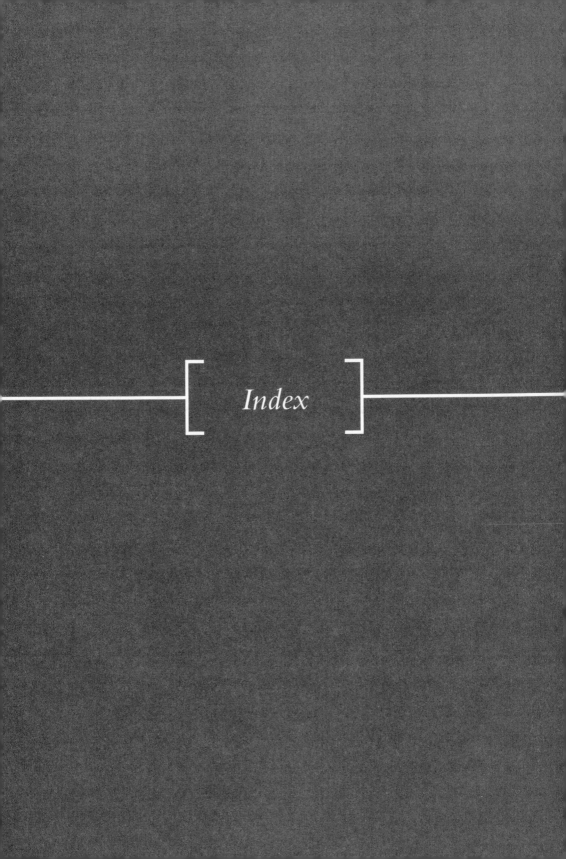

Index

[C]

[D]

[E]

[F]

[U]

[W]

[Z]

Joe John Duran is a three-time author and founding partner of United Capital, which consistently ranks as one of the nation's fastest-growing wealth counseling firms. He previously served as president of GE Private Asset Management. From CNBC to CNN, Joe regularly provides financial commentary on TV. He has been profiled in numerous publications, including the *New York Times* and *SmartMoney*. Joe holds the Chartered Financial Analyst (CFA) designation and earned MBA degrees from Columbia University and UC Berkeley. He lives in Laguna Beach, California, with his wife, Jennifer, and their three precious daughters.